Echoes of Heather and Stone

STOLENSTITCHES.COM

Welcome

Ireland is a small nation, on a small island, but with a rich history and geography that has inspired artists and crafters for generations. Ireland's landscape blends wild sea cliffs, gentle rolling hills, sheltered river valleys, and prickly hedgerows. Ireland's history is a rich tapestry of stone and bronze, of shepherds and chieftains, of Celts and Vikings, and more.

For this book, I invited seven talented designers to draw inspiration from this deep well of living heritage. I didn't want to produce just another book of Aran sweaters. I wanted designs inspired by Ireland on a deeper level, combined with each designer's personality and aesthetic to become something beautifully unique.

For some, this inspiration is very literal and direct; you can immediately see the starting and end point in the design. For others, it is more subtle; a shape, a mood, an echo, that points to the historical roots of the designer's path. In the introduction, Nadia Seaver provides wonderful insights into the inspiration behind the designs, and we also learn, in each designer's own words, about their personal creative process.

Many of the designs in this book are inspired by Ireland's deep history; an Ireland of stone and bronze and ancient spiral carvings, lonely crannogs, weighty dolmans and mysterious passage tombs. Other designs are born out of Ireland's medieval traditions; illuminated texts (the most famous being *The Book Of Kells*) and intricate high crosses. Some are untouched by human endeavor at all, inspired simply by Ireland herself, and her endless verdant fields of clover.

Whatever the inspiration, each pattern is unique and stunning. This talented team of designers have created a collection that you will love to knit and cherish to wear. Enjoy this unique collection of beautiful designs, created by a wonderful team of collaborators.

We hope you find Ireland's heritage as fascinating and inspiring as we did!

Contents

Introduction

By Nadia Seaver

Is there anything as magical as Ireland's Ancient East?

Even today, Ireland's rich history can be seen across our landscape, ancient routes used for trade, networks of passage tombs, standing stones and stone circles can all be visited and enjoyed. This is a land rich in myths, magic, and fairy tales, woven into the stories of old, passed on from parent to child in front of roaring fires on chilly nights. This is a land of High Kings and heroes that can't help but capture the imagination and ignite the creativity within.

Nothing is quite as breathtaking as those monuments that make up Brú na Bóinne (Bend of the Boyne); the tumuli of Newgrange, Knowth and Dowth. Newgrange has captured my imagination ever since I was a child. Constructed about 5,200 years ago, Newgrange is older than Stonehenge and the Great Pyramids of Giza. An enormous circular mound surrounded by ninety seven kerbstones with megalithic art that hosts a twenty-one yard passage that opens out into a chamber with three alcoves. But this is more than just a passage tomb. This was a place of great astronomical, spiritual, religious and ceremonial importance, a place where we said goodbye to our High Kings, welcomed the harvest, and celebrated life.

It is no wonder that this is the area that captured the imagination of Scottish designer Lucy Hague, who's deep love of prehistoric art led to the Newgrange Shawl Design and it's mesmerizing circular patterns.

Lucy tells us about her passion for prehistoric art and her design inspiration and evolution:

Newgrange Shawl by Lucy Hague

"My interest in prehistoric art began in my childhood in Orkney, an island group in the north of Scotland known for its archaeological treasures. I was fortunate to grow up in a landscape where five-thousand year old stone circles, tombs and henges were as familiar to me as roads, schools and farm buildings. This led to an enduring fascination with the art and architecture of the Neolithic period, and inspired me to seek out similar sites elsewhere in the British Isles and across Europe. Along the coastal areas and islands of Western Europe, there appears to be a link in the style of petroglyphic art found at sites such as Achnabreck and Skara Brae in Scotland, Gavrinis in Brittany and Newgrange in Ireland.
Spirals and circles are amongst the oldest symbols, and have

been used in abstract art across the world since prehistoric times. What these symbols meant to the people who carved them has been lost and can never be known for sure, but their beauty and order is still entrancing to modern eyes. Cup-and-ring marks (concentric rings, paired with deeply hollowed out cup shapes, reminiscent of drops of water rippling out) adorn megaliths and natural rock formations at sites all over Britain and Ireland. The spiral is more geometrically complex and has been theorised to represent the procession of the solar cycle throughout the year, and the balance and slow unwinding of the equinoxes and solstices. Numerous spiral carvings decorate the passage tomb of Newgrange, which was designed and built with an orientation towards the winter solstice.

It has been theorised that these symbols could be depictions of entoptic phenomena - the strange shapes and patterns that we 'see' when the flow of our visual perception is temporarily reversed and signals are sent from the visual cortex to the retina. The regularity of these shapes and patterns is remarkably consistent across cultures, and can be predicted to appear under certain conditions, suggesting that we are in effect 'seeing' the very structures of our own visual processing at work.

When I look at the rock art of Newgrange and other similar sites, I also see a deep fascination with numbers, geometry and the repeating, scalable patterns of nature. The tightly wound whorls found in these works could represent fingerprints, spiralling smoke, whirlpools, cloud formations, snail shells, the constant wheeling of the sun, moon and stars through the sky over the course of a year - or all of these things at once, perhaps, a stylised mapping of the underlying patterns of nature. The spiral can also be thought of as a labyrinth, designed to be gazed at and contemplated upon, maybe even as an aid to meditation. The triple spiral in the innermost chamber at Newgrange can be seen as a basic maze - if the negative space between the carved lines of the spiral is taken to be a path it can be followed to the exit with a few different solutions, only one of which traverses the entirety of the spiral.

The double-spiral motif I used in this design traces a path that winds alternatively clockwise and anti-clockwise across its length. The spirals at Newgrange are based on similar double-spiral units. The patterns that fill in the edges of the spirals and create straight edges for the separate panels are inspired by rectilinear shapes found at Newgrange, and also on a carved rock from Orkney known as the Westray Stone - this stone in particular has been noted for its striking similarity to the carvings found at Newgrange."

- Lucy Hague

As we move from Newgrange to Knowth, there is a striking difference in the size of the tombs and the increase of decorative art. Both sites maintain an eerie stillness but Knowth - with its series of eight-century inscriptions within the tomb passages and chambers - is particularly captivating.

Knowth has the longest megalithic passage in Europe and houses a quarter of Western European Neolithic art. All of this was constructed at a time when everything was carefully and laboriously made by hand. Each stroke and carving permanently recorded. I often think of the careful thought process that went into the construction of both the tombs and works of art. How long it would have taken and by how many?

Designer Karie Westermann was also captivated by Knowth, and in her own words describes how its strong geometric lines are represented in her Knowth Shawl design:

Knowth Shawl by Karie Westermann

"Pre-historic stone carvings speak eloquently about the passage of time. Not only have they survived for millennia, but their making was a slow process. They were carved by careful hands using what we'd consider primitive tools.

I have always loved such carvings. As a child I would let my fingers skim local rock art, imagining what it would be like to live several millennia ago. These days I know better than to touch ancient artefacts, but in my imagination I am still reaching out and touching the past. My makers' hands are no different to the stone carvers' hands. My tools and craft may be different, but I am as human as the person who carved an image into a rock so many years ago.

The carved stone at Knowth captures the passage of time. It was carved approximately 5,000 years ago by patient hands; it is slightly weather-worn by millennia of sunshine, rain, and storms; and it was probably intended as a sun-dial. I like how this single carving contains both the brief moment of a day, the careful creative expression carried out over weeks or months, and the long stretch between then and now. Three expressions of time in one beautiful piece.

It became an obvious source of inspiration for a knitted shawl. The Knowth shawl is less a straightforward interpretation of the stone – although its half-circle shape and strong geometric lines obviously lend themselves to knitwear design – but more a meditation upon what time and mark-making mean to a knitter. Garter stitch is easy to knit, but its meditative rhythm is interrupted by slipped stitches that stack to form etchings on top of the knitted fabric. An almost-hourglass-like cable also nods to marking time and its relative complexity asks that the knitter slow down.

Making things takes time and this is ancient knowledge."

- Karie Westermann

In all three sites of Newgrange, Knowth and Dowth you will be drawn to the rhythmic spiral art. These double, or running, spirals have a connecting space between the two vortexes that author Jill Purce describes as symbolizing the opening of the womb, or the division between life and death, and between death and rebirth. Others see it as a visual representation of polarising forces such as good and evil, or sun and moon.

It is this element that inspired the Epona Cowl by Carol Feller, the last design within this book inspired by Brú na Bóinne. Carol describes why these spirals captured her imagination and why colourwork was a perfect choice for this design:

Epona Cowl by Carol Feller

"I've had a lifelong love of spiral motifs and curves. When I doodle it's always spirals. This has in turn drawn me to the wonderful stone art of the Neolithic period. The interlocking spirals carved in stone are a perfect extension of the natural stone form. They create a raised textured surface with each spiral neatly interlocking with the next. As I work in textiles rather than stone I wanted to echo the feel of these stone spirals in the knitting. I opted to do it with colourwork, using colours with subtle contrast for a more subdued effect. The spirals are kept smaller for a more delicate motif and curve backwards and forwards alternating between contrasting colours."

- Carol Feller

r eyes and think of
do you see?"

Each designer within this book has been inspired by the past. Each developing her own creation from a piece of history that caught her eye. Something unique that spoke to them or stayed with them for a few days. For others it was finding something they loved in the designs of the past.

It is no secret that designer Woolly Wormhead has an infectious love of circles, but her inspiration for Trittico is based more on repetition and mathematics than the circular structure of the Celtic cross. Here she describes why the Celtic cross was the basis of the Trittico Hat design:

Wanting to recreate the symbolism of these forms, I deliberately went with 3 motifs around the Hat that are connected by a continuous slipped stitch line that circles the entire Hat. Each motif is marked by a vertical line, from the crown to the brim, that intersects the horizontal line at even points, creating the cross-linked design. The vertical line was a little harder to achieve and it adds a surprising twist!

This feature of using geometry to create the symbolism sits perfectly with the sideways construction of the Hat and the techniques and maths involved."

- Woolly Wormhead

Trittico Hat by Woolly Wormhead

"The inspiration for this design came from the religious artefacts found in historical Ireland, namely, simple Celtic crosses and the intriguing recurrence of items in groups or multiples of three.

When you close your eyes and think of Ireland, what do you see?

When Ireland is mentioned the image that immediately jumps to mind for many are rich green fields, fresh breezes and rolling hills. For me, the Irish countryside has always been a place of retreat. A space filled with a quiet beauty that allows the mind to wander and awaken the artist inside.

Retreats nourish an artists soul and Ireland has a few in breathtaking locations, each with its own unique beauty; a remote island beaten by the elements, a log cabin in the remote hills of Donegal, or a modern artist's retreat in the green hills of Kerry.

In harmony with this spirit, and using one of our famous heritage symbols, Justyna Lorkowska created a jumper that is perfect for wrapping yourself in while exploring Glendalough or braving the elements at the Cliffs of Moher. Justyna tells us why the shamrock is a part of Ireland that·sparked her creative design:

Shamrock Sweater by Justyna Lorkowska

"...Where'er they pass, a triple grass shoots up, with dew-drops streaming,
As softly green as emeralds seen through purest crystal gleaming...
From "Oh, The Shamrock" by Thomas More"

"Long before the poet penned this sentimental verse in the early 19th century, the shamrock held a certain allure for the Irish. Indeed, since ancient times plains blanketed in flowering clover are said to have beckoned St. Brigid to County Kildare, and a shamrock-laden countryside provides a lush, emerald contrast to the dramatic and harsh coastline of the beautiful island of Eire.

The term shamrock comes from an Irish word simply meaning "little plant," and botanically speaking it refers to a variety a three-leaved species, most often a type of clover. Over centuries this tiny floral has become a mighty symbol, attributed not only to St. Patrick and Ireland but to scores of organisations around the world.

This pullover sweater mimics the irresistible softness of Ireland's verdant clover fields and incorporates a delicately subtle cable design reminiscent of the more pronounced Aran stitch patterns long associated with Irish sweaters. The dropped shoulders, relaxed fit and generous cowl are all intended to be casual and comforting – a lovely sweater for wandering the moors or snuggling in."

- Justyna Lorkowska

When I think of Ireland's past, I always think of the lore that has grown up around our stone carvings and what the truth was in their carvings. Some carvings surrounding and engulfing older lines and notches, each one made with great care by a person wishing to leave their mark and tell the world their story.

For Jennifer Wood, the design inspiration for the Ahenny Sweater came from the High Cross, a revered structure from our history. Jennifer guides us through her thought process of her garment design and explains the careful thought that went into her cable choice:

Ahenny Sweater by Jennifer Wood

"High Crosses are considered by some to be Ireland's biggest contribution to Western European Art of the Middle Ages. Although I do not know a lot about Ireland's art history, I do know that the High Crosses are enchanting. They are stone storytellers, their outstretched arms recording old and new testament stories entwined with the Celtic story. Looking at the bands that are spiraled, braided, and knotted in complex geometric patterns, I can imagine that cable knitting was created to carry on the beauty of High Crosses.

These beautiful crosses inspired my design. While planning the design, I knew that I did not want to copy a pattern from a cross but wanted to create one that would be a reflection of the crosses—a pattern to delight the eye in the same way. I also knew that although cables would be the best way to reflect the intricate designs on the crosses, I did not want to use a traditional cabled sweater.

Keeping this in mind as I searched through cable patterns, I finally chose a large border cable, which is based on Norah Gaughan's Swing Diamonds cable pattern from Knitted Cable Sourcebook, and some circle cables, which I manipulated to fit the needs of the design. Because the border cable has a cross shape, it was a good starting point for the front. The cables that create the border swing in and out and around each other, reflecting the spiraling bands on the crosses. For a delicate intricacy, I embedded the circle cable within the border cable.

The circle-within-a-circle cable pattern on the back reflects the arms of the cross that are often linked by a circle. The alternating pattern makes a perfect panel for the back of the sweater. To further reflect the curved carvings, the Stockinette stitches curve in and out, following the shape of the cables.

For the sleeves, I at first thought about running a single circle cable down the center, but it did not work the way I imagined, so I took the middle section out of the border cable and altered the size to fit on the sleeves. Then, embedding the rope cable within the border, I carried the it down the sleeve—perfect. The embedded and entwined curves continued down the sleeve reflect the entwined strands reaching down the arms of High Crosses. To add to that reflection, I used another rope cable beginning at the under arm and curving around to the front of the sweater, adding a pretty reverse-Stockinette stitch pattern to finish the bottom and sleeves.

That just left the neckline. Initially, I was going to add a decorative neck band, but while finishing the sweater, I realized simple would be prettiest, reflecting the simple material of the stone. Together, these designs create a sweater that is steeped in the beautiful history of the High Crosses, but made fresh by interesting cable patterns and modern shaping.

I named the sweater Ahenny, after the two ringed Ahenny High Crosses. Ahenny is a small village nestled on the lovely slopes of Carrigadoon Hill overlooking a valley in County Tipperary. Near to the village is the early Christian foundation of Kilclispeen monastery, and in the adjoining graveyard stand the two crosses, thought to be among the earliest examples of Celtic High Crosses in Ireland.

- Jennifer Wood

We all want to feel connected.

We need to know where we came from and to explore our family's origins. Understanding our family tree, being able to relate backwards in time with those who took part in famous deeds and battles, adds meaning to our lives in the present Our ancestors, who lived so long ago, can still inspire us today.

What we create also touches our past, present and our future Making has meaning, Each stitch contains a part of ourselves. Each piece tells a story of its own, if you listen closely enough.

For Amanda Schwabe, it is this connection that takes center stage in her design. Amanda kindly describes why connections are so important to her, and how cables were the perfect medium to create her relaxed cardigan:

Talamed Cardigan by Amanda Schwabe

"The wonderfully strange thing about knitting is that it's a series of strings that have been connected by bending loops and pulling more loops through them to hold them in place, and so on. It's crazy and yet completely sane, and it works even when we don't fully understand what's happening. It feels like a small miracle unfolding in our hands, and people have been doing this for years with whatever sticks and string they could make. This is how we keep ourselves warm, how we keep ourselves calm and comforted inside and out.

We, today, knit in an unbroken line that flows from times we can't remember. But we can see the connection in glimpses of the past carved into stones or intricately doodled on holy texts, messages from the past sent forward to remind us: we are all connected. Our lives intertwine with the past, present, and future; with each person we smile or frown at each day; with every message we write in a bottle or a sweater. Everything cascades and flows together, and we can't escape this connection. Every stitch in these cables moves inexorably towards its crossing point, which affects the next crossing, and so on. Over, under, over, under.... Everything in knitting and in life is a chance to grow, to learn, to rip out and try again. So get inspired, knit someone a cozy hug, and make the world a little better with your sticks and string. It really does matter. We're all connected.

Talamed is a long, cozy cardigan with over-sized collar and front bands that you can wear belted and overlapping, folded and pinned under the collar, or open and flowing. Fold the reversible collar under instead of out for a different look, or even leave it up and slightly scrunched. The background stripes blend heathered Nua colours in unexpected ways, and the swirling, intertwining lines that decorate the surface highlight each colour to make it stand out. Choose a contrasting front edging and cuffs like we did, or stick with two colours throughout for a different, more subtle look."

- Amanda Schwabe

Our Ancestors liked to tell stories. They harnessed the power that lay in their imagination, turning them into works of art that are still enjoyed in the present day. They warned of love and its consequences, of the fair folk (faeries) and respect, of courage, and of the power of being underestimated. Sometimes they used symbols, like the spirals we looked at previously, and sometimes they used runes, in which each mark held deep meaning and took time to create.

One of our most ancient written systems is Ogham, a medieval alphabet used to capture the early Irish language. Many still believe that these runes hold power but the design of the runes you see throughout Ireland are captivating to look at.

It is these inscriptions that caught the eye of designer Isabell Kraemer which led to the yoked garment, Áine. This is a beautiful design that almost feels like you are adorning yourself with ancient art, wearing the colourwork like a jewel, while still being comfortable and relaxed to wear. Isabell describes where her inspiration for the garment came from:

Áine Sweater by Isabell Kraemer

"Ireland has such a rich history and I wanted to reflect some of its culture in this sweater design. My aim was to create a contemporary design that recognised the geometric lines and shapes of the ancient Celtic symbols. My idea was to design a torc-like yoke (necklace) incorporating some of the stylised and energetic circular forms of Celtic runes but with a more modern (current) twist. With Áine I hope I have achieved this.

- Isabell Kraemer

From our quiet countryside to engravings of our past, the designers within this collection have created pieces that represent what ancient Ireland means to them. By discussing the design inspiration behind each piece, from the choices in cables and colourwork, you can see each unique piece evolving and forming organically to create a beautifully striking garment or accessory. Upon making them, I hope you capture your own piece of history, knitted into each design.

What story will you tell?

- Nadia Seaver

Newgrange
by Lucy Hague

SIZES

One Size

FINISHED MEASUREMENTS

Shawl Width: 54" / 137 cm
Shawl Depth: 27" / 68.5 cm
Each spiral measures 7˝ / 18 cm diameter after joining and blocking.

YARN

Stolen Stitches 'Nua' (60% Merino, 20% Linen, 20% Yak, 153 yds / 140 m per 1.76 oz / 50 g); **Colour:** Kitten Fluff (9810), 5 skeins;
Approx Yardage Used: 685 yds / 626 m

NEEDLES & NOTIONS

US size 5 / 3.75 mm circular needle, at least 32"/ 80 cm long (to work and hold Panel 1)
US size 5 / 3.75 mm circular needle, at least 47"/ 120 cm long (to work and hold Panel 2)
US size 5 / 3.75 mm circular needle, at least 59"/ 150 cm long (to work and hold Panel 3)
US size 5 / 3.75 mm dpns (at least 15 cm long) or short/medium circular needle (for knitting spirals and working edging)

Always use a needle size that gives you the gauge listed, as every knitter's gauge is unique.

22 stitch markers, safety pins, tapestry needle, darning needle, cable needle, waste yarn

GAUGE

21.5 sts / 30.5 rows = 4"/ 10 cm in St St blocked

ABBREVIATIONS

See Abbreviations Section on Page 74.

TECHNIQUES & STITCH PATTERNS

See Techniques Section on Page 75 for any additional techniques not detailed in pattern.

1-into-3

On RS: Insert rn between first 2 sts on ln, wrap yarn and pull through, sl first st on ln to rn; insert ln between first 2 sts on rn, wrap yarn around ln as though to make k st, pull yarn through, sl st just created to rn. 1 st increased to 3 sts.
On WS: Purl into front of st, yo, purl into back of same st.
https://stolenstitches.com/blogs/tutorials/increase-1-into-3

1-into-5

Insert rn between first 2 sts on ln, wrap yarn and pull through, sl first st on ln to rn; insert ln between first 2 sts on rn, wrap yarn around ln as though to make k st, pull yarn through, sl first st on rn back to ln.
Repeat instructions between asterisks once, sl st just created to rn, sl rem sts on ln to rn. 1 st increased to 5 sts.
https://stolenstitches.com/blogs/tutorials/increase-1-into-5

2/1 LPC

Sl next 2 sts to cn and hold to front, p1, k2 from cn.

2/1 RPC

Sl next st to cn and hold to back, k2, p1 from cn.

2/2 LPC

Sl next 2 sts to cn and hold to front, p2, k2 from cn.

2/2 RPC

Sl next 2 sts to cn and hold to back, k2, p2 from cn.

p2sl1psso

RS: P2tog, sl st to ln wyif, pass second st on ln over st just slipped, sl st back to rn.

sl1k2psso

WS: Sl st to rn wyib, k2tog, pass second st on rn over st just worked.

Charts

Use either written or charted directions. All written directions for these charts are available in the electronic version of the book.

PATTERN NOTES

This shawl is worked modularly. First 9 spirals are worked, then joined together. Stitches are picked up around the spirals and short rows are worked to fill in the gaps between the spirals and create 3 separate rectangular panels. After the third panel is worked, one of the edges of the shawl is cast off with a lace edging, then an edging is worked across the top of the shawl whilst at the same time, the spiral panels are joined with panels of plain knitting. Finally, the remaining edge of the shawl is cast off with a lace edging to match the opposite side.

This pattern makes use of short rows; when working back over areas with wrapped stitches, remember to pick up and work the wrap so that it is hidden at the back of the work. For example, when working wrap on the RS, if in an area of stocking stitch, lift wrap and k2tog with parent st; if in an area of reverse stocking stitch, lift wrap and p2tog with parent st. When working wrap on the WS, if in an area of stocking stitch on RS, lift wrap and ssp with parent st.

SCHEMATIC

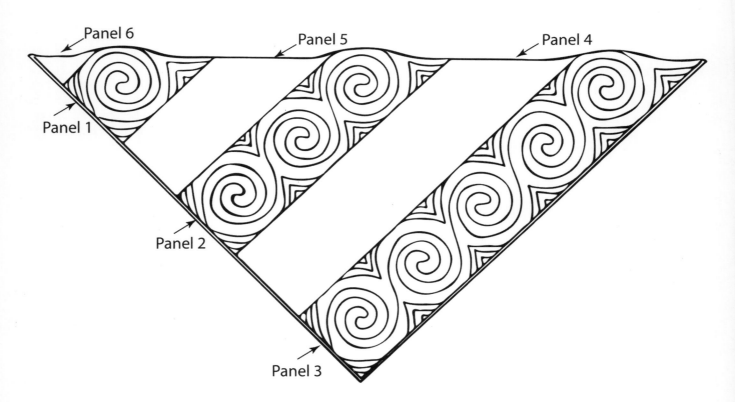

Spiral Chart A

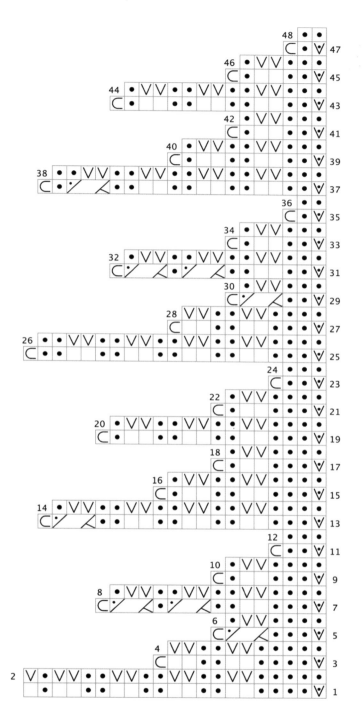

Spiral Chart B

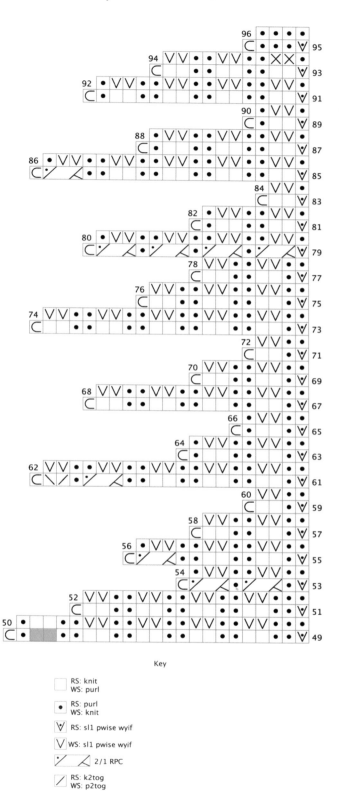

Key

	RS: knit WS: purl
•	RS: purl WS: knit
V̇	RS: sl1 pwise wyif
V	WS: sl1 pwise wyif
⟍⟋	2/1 RPC
⟋	RS: k2tog WS: p2tog
⟍	RS: ssk WS: p2tog tbl
XX	Sl 2 sts to safety pin, CO 2 sts w/ Backwards Loop CO
▨	refer to written instructions
C	w&t

Chart C

Key

- RS: knit / WS: purl
- RS: purl / WS: knit
- RS: p1 tbl
- 1-into-3: see notes
- 1-into-5: see notes
- WS: sl1 pwise wyif
- 2/1 RPC
- 2/1 LPC
- 2/2 RPC
- 2/2 LPC
- RS: ssp
- RS: p2tog / WS: k2tog
- RS: p2sl1psso / WS: sl1k2psso
- WS: ssp
- RS: k2tog
- RS: RLI / WS: LLIp
- grey no stitch
- w&t
- w&t

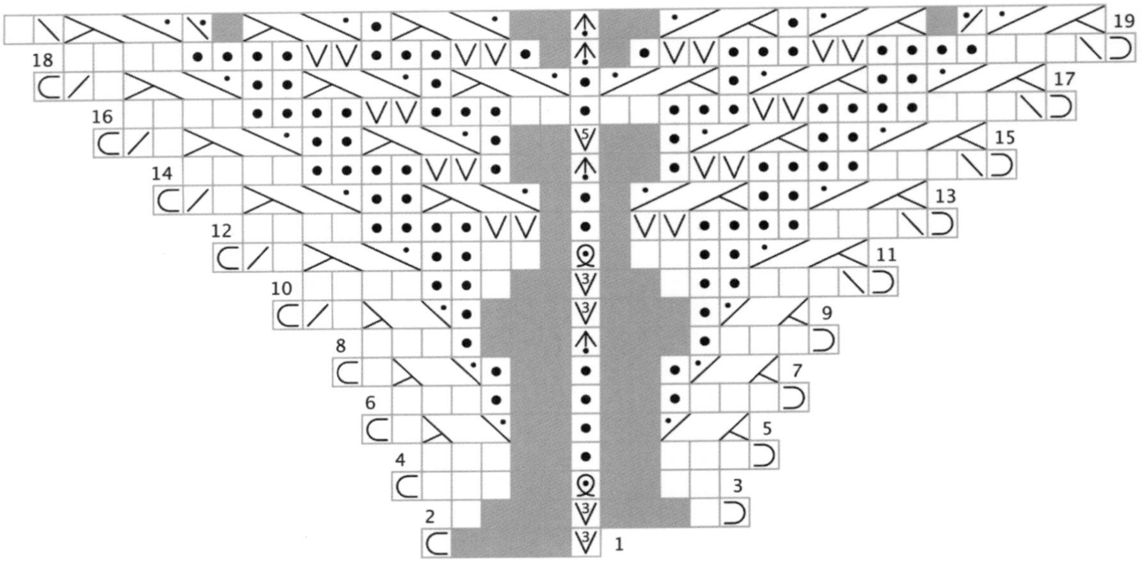

Chart C [Edge]

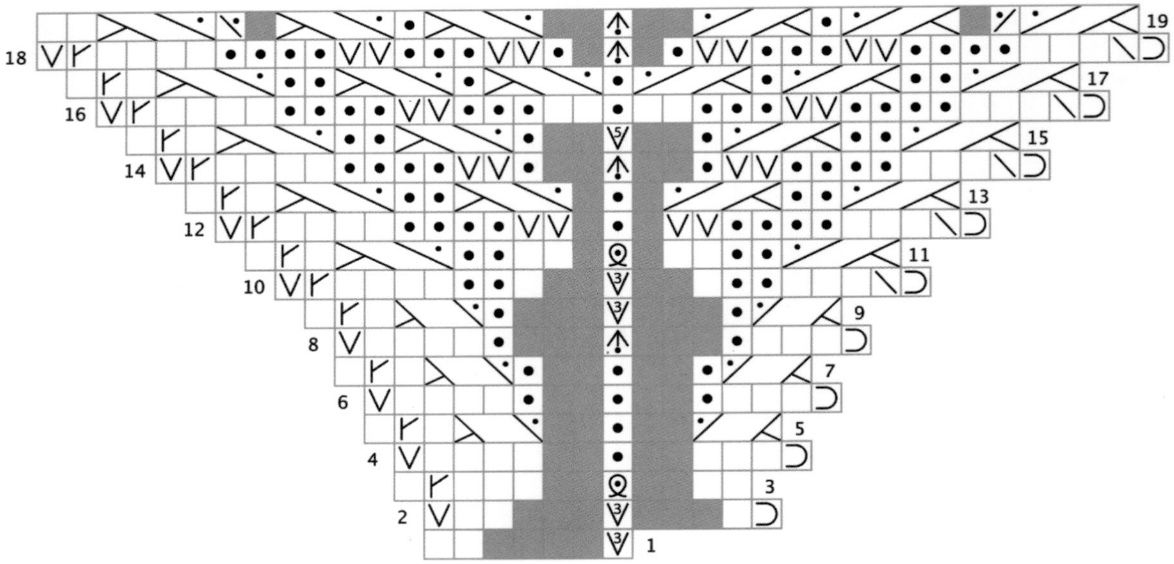

Chart D

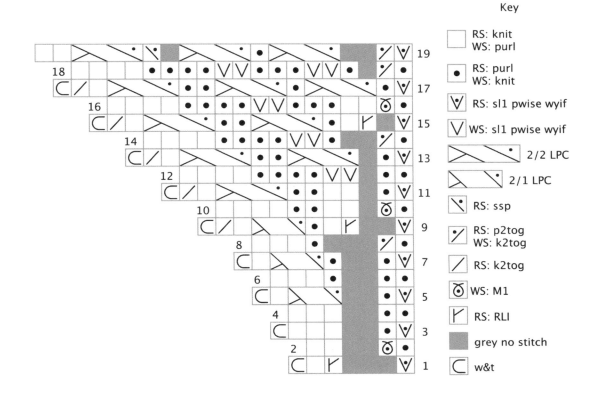

Key

	RS: knit
□	WS: purl
•	RS: purl
	WS: knit
V̌	RS: sl1 pwise wyif
V	WS: sl1 pwise wyif
⟋•	2/2 LPC
⟋•	2/1 LPC
\•	RS: ssp
⟋•	RS: p2tog
	WS: k2tog
⟋	RS: k2tog
⊘	WS: M1
⊢	RS: RLI
▨	grey no stitch
⊂	w&t

Chart E

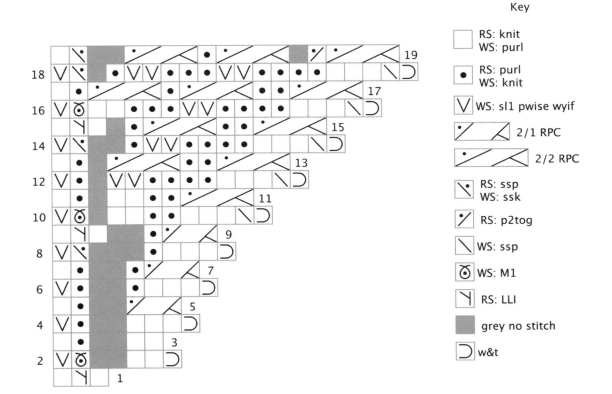

Key

	RS: knit
□	WS: purl
•	RS: purl
	WS: knit
V	WS: sl1 pwise wyif
•⟋ ⟍	2/1 RPC
•⟋ ⟍	2/2 RPC
\•	RS: ssp
	WS: ssk
⟋•	RS: p2tog
\	WS: ssp
⊘	WS: M1
⊢	RS: LLI
▨	grey no stitch
⊃	w&t

PATTERN

Work Spirals

Spiral Chart A shows Rows 1-48. Spiral Chart B shows Rows 49-96. Work all short row wraps with the st they wrap as you pass.

To work one spiral:

Using Invisible Provisional Cast-On with waste yarn, and 2 dpns or 1 short circ needle, CO 21 sts, leaving a working yarn tail of approx. 15" / 38 cm at beginning of cast on (this will be used to graft the spiral together).

Turn and work Row 2 of Spiral Chart/Written Instructions. Work Rows 3-48.

Row 49 (RS): Sl1 wyif, [p2, k2] 4 times, p2, cast on 2 sts using backwards loop cast-on, [sl 2 sts back to ln, k2] twice, p1, w&t. *23 sts.*

Work Rows 50- 96 of Spiral Chart/Written Instructions.
Work Rows 1-96 once more to complete the second half of the spiral; when working Row 49 on the repeat, instead of casting on 2 sts, use ln to lift the base of the 2 sts previously cast on to the ln, pick up and knit 2 sts in the base of these sts (this creates the join at the centre of the spiral).
Work Row 1 once more; break yarn at end of this row.

Spiral Grafting

Slide sts to opposite end of needle, so that the needle-tip is positioned at the beginning of the RS row. With other dpn/other end of circ needle, sl provisionally cast-on sts from waste yarn to needle, from the inside to outside of the spiral, being careful to make sure that sts are oriented correctly (with right leg of st at front of needle, and left leg of st at back of needle). *21 sts on both needle-tips.*

Turn work back so that last worked row is facing, and using working yarn tail left at beginning of provisional cast-on at outer edge of spiral, thread onto a darning needle and bring yarn in between stitch 1 and stitch 2 on back needle.

In the following grafting instructions, 'knit' or 'purl' refers to inserting the darning needle knitwise or purlwise through the st, respectively (pull yarn all the way through st after inserting darning needle); 'on' or 'off' refers to leaving the st on the needle or letting it slip off; 'Front' and 'Back' refer to the needles as they appear to you (i.e. front needle is the needle closest to you).

Graft last row and first row together in pattern as follows:
Front: purl on
Back: knit on
Front: knit off, knit on
Back: knit off, purl on

Graft all the way across, using the following instructions according to which 2 sts are next on the front needle (reading sts from right to left):

If next 2 sts on front needle are 2 purl sts:
Front: purl off, knit on
Back: knit off, purl on

If next 2 sts on front needle are 1 purl st, then 1 knit st:
Front: purl off, purl on
Back: purl off, knit on

If next 2 sts on front needle are 2 knit sts:
Front: knit off, purl on
Back: purl off, knit on

If next 2 sts on front needle are 1 knit st, then 1 purl st:
Front: knit off, knit on
Back: knit off, purl on

When one st remains on each needle, work as follows:
Front: purl off
Back: knit off

Draw yarn tail through centre of spiral to WS and weave ends in securely.

Work another 8 identical spirals (9 in total).

Work Panel 1

1 spiral

Beginning at approx. 1" / 2.5 cm above sts held on safety pin, with RS facing and using medium length circ needle, join in yarn and pick up and knit 22 sts along spiral edge, to mid-point of spiral, pm.

Pick up and knit 22 sts from mid-point of spiral to approx. 1" / 2.5 cm before sts held on safety pin. Pick up and knit 3 sts to sts held on safety pin, sl 2 sts from safety pin to ln and k2, pick up and knit 3 sts, pm, pick up and knit 22 sts to mid-point of spiral, pm.

Pick up and knit 22 sts from mid-point of spiral to approx. 1" / 2.5 cm before sts held on safety pin. Pick up and knit 3 sts, sl 2 sts from safety pin to ln and k2, pick up and knit 3 sts to beginning of picked up sts. *104 sts.*

With RS facing, work Chart D. There are 18 sts to first marker after completing Chart D. After Row 19 of Chart D, k20, work Chart C [Edge]. Note after working each instance of Chart C and Chart C [Edge] st count in each section is 33 sts (31 sts from chart, plus 2 sts at beginning of section).

After Row 19 of Chart C [Edge], with RS facing pick up and knit 10 sts along edge of section just worked, k7 to marker, k22 to marker; k20, work Chart E.

After Row 19 of Chart E, with RS facing pick up and knit 10 sts along edge of section just worked, k8, pick up and knit 10 sts along edge of first section worked. Break yarn and sl 28 sts just worked to waste yarn.

With RS facing, sl 51 sts from longest edge of Panel 1 to rn. Sl 28 sts from top edge of strip (Chart C [Edge]) to a separate piece of waste yarn; leave next 29 sts on circ needle. Both needle tips are now positioned at the top of the panel.

Work Panel 2

3 spirals

To join 2 spirals:

Position 2 spirals next to each other so that sts held on safety pins line up. Sl sts from safety pins to dpns (2 sts on each dpn). With a new length of yarn (approx. 16" / 40.5 cm), graft these sts together, leaving an 8" / 20.5 cm length at beginning of graft. After sts have been grafted, use mattress st to seam sides of spirals together along the slipped st edge of each spiral, for a length of approx. 3 slipped sts. Return to beginning of graft and use mattress st to seam sides of spiral together as before.

Join a total of 3 spirals together to create a strip (leave sts held on safety pins at beginning and end of strip).

Beginning at one end of strip, approx. 1" / 2.5 cm above sts held on safety pin, with RS facing and using long circular needle, join in yarn and pick up and knit 22 sts along spiral edge, to mid-point of first spiral, pm.

[Pick up and knit 20 sts along remaining edge of spiral, pick up and knit 1 st in centre of join between spirals, pick up and knit 20 sts to mid-point of next spiral, pm] twice.

Pick up and knit 22 sts from mid-point of spiral to approx. 1" / 2.5 cm before sts held on safety pin. Pick up and knit 3 sts to sts held on safety pin, sl 2 sts from safety pin to ln and k2, pick up and knit 3 sts, pm; pick up and knit 22 sts to mid-point of spiral, pm.

[Pick up and knit 20 sts along remaining edge of spiral, pick up and knit 1 st in centre of join between spirals, pick up and knit 20 sts to mid-point of next spiral, pm] twice.

Pick up and knit 22 sts from mid-point of spiral to approx. 1" / 2.5 cm before sts held on safety pin. Pick up and knit 3 sts, sl 2 sts from safety pin to ln and k2, pick up and knit 3 sts to beginning of picked up sts. *268 sts.*

With RS facing, work Chart D. After Row 19 of Chart D, [k20, work Chart C] twice, k20, work Chart C [Edge].

After Row 19 of Chart C [Edge], with RS facing pick up and knit

10 sts along edge of section just worked, k7 to marker, k22 to marker; [k20, work Chart C] twice; k20, work Chart E.

After Row 19 of Chart E, with RS facing, pick up and knit 10 sts along edge of section just worked, k8, pick up and knit 10 sts along edge of first section worked. Break yarn and sl 28 sts just worked to waste yarn.

With RS facing, sl 117 sts from longest edge of Panel 2 to rn. Sl 28 sts from top edge of strip to a separate piece of waste yarn; leave next 95 sts on circ needle. Both needle tips are now positioned at the top of the panel.

Work Panel 3

5 spirals

Join rem 5 spirals together to create a strip (leave sts held on safety pins at beginning and end of strip).

Beginning at one end of strip, approx. 1" / 2.5 cm above sts held on safety pin, with RS facing and using longest circ needle, join in yarn and pick up and knit 22 sts along spiral edge, to mid-point of first spiral, pm.

[Pick up and knit 20 sts along remaining edge of spiral, pick up and knit 1 st in centre of join between spirals, pick up and knit 20 sts to mid-point of next spiral, pm] 4 times.

Pick up and knit 22 sts from mid-point of spiral to approx. 1" / 2.5 cm before sts held on safety pin. Pick up and knit 3 sts to sts held on safety pin, sl 2 sts from safety pin to ln and k2, pick up and knit 3 sts, pm, pick up and knit 22 sts to mid-point of spiral, pm.

[Pick up and knit 20 sts along remaining edge of spiral, pick up and knit 1 st in centre of join between spirals, pick up and knit 20 sts to mid-point of next spiral, pm] 4 times.

Pick up and knit 22 sts from mid-point of spiral to approx. 1" / 2.5 cm before sts held on safety pin. Pick up and knit 3 sts, sl 2 sts from safety pin to ln and k2, pick up and knit 3 sts to beginning of picked up sts. *432 sts.*

With RS facing, work Chart D.

After Row 19 of Chart D, [k20, work Chart C] 4 times; k20, work Chart C [Edge].

After Row 19 of Chart C [Edge], pm and with RS facing pick up and knit 10 sts along edge of section just worked, k7 to marker, k22 to marker, [k20, work Chart C] 4 times, k20, work Chart E.

After Row 19 of Chart E, with RS facing, pick up and knit 10 sts along edge of section just worked, k8, pick up and knit 10 sts along edge of first section worked. Sl 28 sts just worked to waste yarn.

Work Edging Along Side of Panel 3

Turn work to WS and without breaking yarn at end of slipped sts, CO 5 sts using a provisional cast-on and waste yarn. Turn back to RS and using a dpn as rn, work short rows as follows (pick up and work wraps as they are encountered):

Row 1 (RS): Sl1 wyif, k1, w&t.
Row 2 (WS): P1, k1.
Row 3 (RS): Sl1 wyif, k1, yo, k2tog, w&t.
Row 4 (WS): P3, k1.
Row 5 (RS): Sl1 wyif, k1, yo, k2tog, sssk with sts from circ needle.
Row 6 (WS): Sl1 wyif, p3, k1.

Work lace edging all the way along side of Panel 3 as follows:
Row 1 (RS): Sl1 wyif, k1, yo, k2tog, ssk with st from circ needle. *5 sts.*
Rows 2, 4, and 6 (WS): Sl1 wyif, p3, k1.
Row 3 (RS): Rep Row 1.
Row 5 (RS): Sl1 wyif, k1, yo, k2tog, sssk with sts from circ needle.

Remove markers as they are encountered. Work lace edging as set by last 6 rows until 1 st remains on Panel 3 edge (before marker at top corner of panel). Work final short rows of lace edging as follows:
Row 1 (RS): Sl1 wyif, k1, yo, k2tog, w&t.
Row 2 (WS): P3, k1.
Row 3 (RS): Sl1 wyif, k1, w&t.
Row 4 (WS): P1, k1.
Row 5 (RS): Sl1 wyif, k1, yo, k2tog, ssk with st from circ needle and remove marker.
Row 6 (WS): Sl1 wyif, p3, k1.

With WS still facing, CO 3 sts at end of row using backwards loop cast-on.

Work Edging Across Top of Panel 3

Turn to RS, work Edging across top of Panel 3 as follows:
Row 1 (RS): Sl1 wyif, k2, ssk with st from circ needle.
Row 2 (WS): Sl1 wyif, p2, k1.

Work Edging as set by last 2 rows until first marker is reached, then remove marker and work Edging over next 16 sts on circ needle as follows:
Row 1 (RS): Sl1 wyif, k2, ssk with st from circ needle.
Rows 2, 4 and 6 (WS): Sl1 wyif, p2, k1.
Row 3 (RS): Rep Row 1.
Row 5 (RS): Sl1 wyif, k2, sssk with sts from circ needle.
Work Rows 1-6 a further 3 times. *6 sts rem before next marker.*

Row 1 (RS): Sl1 wyif, k2, ssk with st from circ needle, w&t.
Row 2 (WS): Sl1 wyif, p2, k1.
Row 3 (RS): Sl1 wyif, k3, p2, w&t.
Row 4 (WS): K2, p3, k1.
Row 5 (RS): Sl1 wyif, k3, p2, k1, k2tog, remove marker, w&t.

Row 6 (WS): P2, k2, p3, k1.
33 sts including wrapped st rem before next marker.

Begin Panel 4

Row 1 (RS): Sl1 wyif, k3, M1, p2, k2, ssk with st from circ needle. *10 sts.*
Row 2 (WS): Sl1 wyif, p2, k2, p4, k1.
Row 3 (RS): Sl1 wyif, k3, M1, k1, p2, k2, ssk with st from circ needle. *11 sts.*
Row 4 (WS): Sl1 wyif, p2, k2, p5, k1.
Row 5 (RS): Sl1 wyif, k3, M1, knit to purl sts, p2, k2, ssk with st from circ needle. *12 sts.*
Row 6 (WS): Sl1 wyif, p2, k2, purl to last st, k1.
Row 7 (RS): Sl1 wyif, k3, M1, k1, M1, knit to purl sts, p2, k2, sssk with sts from circ needle. *14 sts.*
Row 8 (WS): Sl1 wyif, p2, k2, purl to last st, k1.
14 sts worked of Panel 4, 28 sts rem to next marker.

*Work Rows 5 & 6 three times, then work Rows 7 & 8 once; rep from * 3 more times.
34 sts worked of Panel 4, 7 sts rem to next marker.
Work Rows 5 & 6 twice more.

Row 1 (RS): Sl1 wyif, k3, M1p, knit to purl sts, p2, k2, ssk with st from circ needle. *37 sts worked, 4 sts rem to next marker.*
Row 2 (WS): Sl1 wyif, p2, k2, purl to last 5 sts, k1, M1, p3, k1. *38 sts.*
Row 3 (RS): Sl1 wyif, k3, M1, p2, knit to purl sts, p2, k2, sssk with sts from circ needle. *39 sts worked, 2 sts rem to next marker.*
Row 4 (WS): Sl1 wyif, p2, k2, purl to last 7 sts, k2, p1, M1p, p3, k1. *40 sts.*
Row 5 (RS): Sl1 wyif, k3, M1, k2, p2, knit to purl sts, p2, k2, sssk with sts from circ needle. *41 sts worked, 0 sts rem to next marker.* Remove marker.
Row 6 (WS): Sl1 wyif, p2, k2, purl to last 9 sts, k2, p3, wrap next st and sl to ln, without turning sl next 4 sts to waste yarn/st holder.

Join Panels 2 and 3, WHILST WORKING PANEL 4

Using circ needle from longer edge of Panel 2 as rn, with RS facing:
Row 1 (RS): Sl1 wyib, k2, p2, k27, p2, k2, ssk.
Row 2 (WS): Sl1 wyif, p2, k2, p27, k2, p2, p2tog.
Row 3 (RS): Rep Row 1.
Row 4 (WS): Rep Row 2.
Row 5 (RS): Rep Row 1.
Row 6 (WS): Rep Row 2.
Row 7 (RS): Sl1 wyif, k2, p2, k27, p2, k2, sssk.
Row 8 (WS): Sl1 wyif, p2, k2, p27, k2, p2, p3tog.
Work these 8 rows until next marker is reached on both sides, remove markers as they are encountered and begin again from Row 1 after removing markers.
Continue until 2 unattached sts remain on each side.
Next Row (RS): Rep Row 7.

Next Row (WS): Rep Row 8.
Break yarn and sl 37 rem sts from Panel 4 onto waste yarn.

Work Edging Across Top of Panel 2

Return to 4 sts held on waste yarn/st holder at top of Panel 4. With nearest end of circ needle, turn to WS and sl 28 sts at top of Panel 2 from waste yarn back to needle, sl held 4 sts from Panel 4 to needle. Join in yarn and work exactly as for edging worked across top of Panel 3.

Begin Panel 5

Work exactly as for beginning of Panel 4.

Join Panels 1 and 2, WHILST WORKING PANEL 5

Using circ needle from longer edge of Panel 1 as rn, join Panels 1 and 2 exactly as for Panels 2 and 3.

Work Edging Across Top of Panel 1

Return to 4 sts held on waste yarn/st holder at top of Panel 5. With nearest end of circ needle, turn to WS and sl 28 sts at top of Panel 1 from waste yarn back to needle, sl held 4 sts from Panel 5 to needle. Join in yarn and work exactly as for edging worked across top of Panel 3.

Note that after this section is worked, there will be 18 sts including wrapped st rem on circ needle.

Begin Panel 6

Work first 8 rows as directed for beginning Panel 4, then *Work Rows 5 & 6 three times, then work Rows 7 & 8; Rep from * one more time.
Work Rows 5 & 6 once.
Next Row (RS): Sl1 wyif, k3, M1, knit to purl sts, p2, k2, sssk with sts from circ needle.
Next Row (WS): Sl1 wyif, p2, k2, purl to last st, k1. *26 sts*;

WORK FINAL EDGING

Begin lace edging by working short rows as follows:
Row 1 (RS): Sl1 wyif, k1, w&t.
Row 2 (WS): P1, k1.
Row 3 (RS): Sl1 wyif, k1, yo, k2tog, w&t.
Row 4 (WS): P3, k1.
Row 5 (RS): Sl1 wyif, k1, yo, k2tog, sssk with sts from circ needle.
Row 6 (WS): Sl1 wyif, p3, k1.

With long circ needle, sl all remaining sts on waste yarn at edge of shawl back to needle.

Work lace edging all the way along edge of shawl as follows:
Row 1 (RS): Sl1 wyif, k1, yo, k2tog, ssk with st from circ needle. *5 sts.*
Row 2 (and all WS rows): Sl1 wyif, p3, k1.

Row 3 (RS): Rep Row 1.
Row 5 (RS): Sl1 wyif, k1, yo, k2tog, sssk with sts from circ needle.
Row 6 (WS): Rep Row 2.
Work lace edging until 1 st remains before provisionally cast-on edge of previously worked lace edging.
Work final short rows of lace edging as follows:
Row 1 (RS): Sl1 wyif, k1, yo, k2tog, w&t.
Row 2 (WS): P3, k1.
Row 3 (RS): Sl1 wyif, k1, w&t.
Row 4 (WS): P1, k1.
Row 5 (RS): Sl1 wyif, k1, yo, k2tog, ssk with st from circ needle.

Turn work to WS. Cut yarn, leaving a length to graft sts together. Remove waste yarn from provisionally cast-on sts and arrange sts on 2 dpns, 5 sts on each needle. Graft sts together using reverse stocking stitch grafting (directions for purl st followed by a purl st).

FINISHING

Weave in all ends.
Soak shawl and block by threading blocking wires through lace edging and pinning out. Pin out top edge, leaving edge to roll under slightly.
Allow to dry completely.

Knowth

by Karie Westermann

SIZES

One Size

FINISHED MEASUREMENTS

Shawl Width: 54.5" / 138.5 cm
Shawl Depth: 22" / 56 cm

YARN

Stolen Stitches 'Nua' (60% Merino, 20% Linen, 20% Yak, 153 yds / 140 m per 1.76 oz / 50g); **Colours: MC:** Bare Necessities (9806), 4 skeins; **CC:** Angry Monkey (9807), 3 skeins; **Approx Yardage Used: MC:** 535 yds / 489 m; **CC:** 382 yds / 350 m

NEEDLES & NOTIONS

US size 7 / 4.5 mm circular needle, 32" / 80 cm long

Always use a needle size that gives you the gauge listed, as every knitter's gauge is unique.

2 markers A, 7 markers B, 8 removable markers C, Tapestry needle, Cable needle

GAUGE

18 sts and 35 rows = 4" / 10 cm in Garter Stitch blocked Edge Chart meas 3.5" / 9 cm across

ABBREVIATIONS

See Abbreviations Section on Page 74.

TECHNIQUES & STITCH PATTERNS

See Techniques Section on Page 75 for any additional techniques not detailed in pattern.

1/1 RC

Slip 1 stitch onto cn and hold in back; k1, then k1 from cn.

1/1 LPC

Slip 1 stitch onto cn and hold in front; p1, then k1 from cn.

1/1 RPC

Slip 1 stitch onto cn and hold in back; k1, then p1 from cn.

2/1 LPC

Slip 2 sts onto cn and hold at front; p1, then k2 from cn.

2/1 RPC

Slip 1 stitch onto cn and hold at back; k2, then p1 from cn.

2/2 RC

Slip 2 sts onto cn and hold in back; k2, then k2 from cn.

1/1/2 LCPK

Slip 2 sts onto cn and hold at front; k1, p1, then k2 from cn.

2/1/1 RCPK

Slip 2 sts onto cn and hold at back; k2, then p1, k1 from cn.

Edge

Use either written or charted directions.

Edge Written Directions

Row 1 (RS): Sl1, p4, ssk, yo, p2, 2/2 RC, p2, yo, k2tog, p5.
Row 2 (WS): Yo, p2tog, k3, p1, k3, p4, k3, p1, k4, k2tog.
Row 3 (RS): Sl1, p4, 1/1 LPC, 2/1/1 RCPK, 1/1/2 LCPK, 1/1 RPC, p5.
Row 4 (WS): Yo, p2tog, k4, p3, k1, p2, k1, p3, k5, k2tog.
Row 5 (RS): Sl1, p5, 2/1 RPC, k2tog, double yo, ssk, 2/1 LPC, p6.
Row 6 (WS): Yo, p2tog, k4, [p2, k1] twice, p1, k1, p2, k5, k2tog.
Row 7 (RS): Sl1, p4, 2/1 RPC, k2tog, yo, 1/1 RC, yo, ssk, 2/1 LPC, p5.
Rows 8 and 10 (WS): Yo, p2tog, k3, p2, k1, p6, k1, p2, k4, k2tog.
Row 9 (RS): Sl1, p4, k2, p1, ssk, yo, 1/1 RC, yo, k2tog, p1, k2, p5.
Row 11 (RS): Sl1, p4, 2/1 LPC, k1, k2tog, double yo, ssk, k1, 2/1 RPC, p5.
Row 12 (WS): Yo, p2tog, k4, p4, [p1 tbl] twice, p4, k5, k2tog.
Row 13 (RS): Sl1, p5, 1/1/2 LCPK, p2, 2/1/1 RCPK, p6.
Row 14 (WS): Yo, p2tog, k4, p1, k1, p2, k2, p2, k1, p1, k5, k2tog.
Row 15 (RS): Sl1, p4, k2tog, yo, p1, 2/1 LPC, 2/1 RPC, p1, yo, ssk, p5.
Row 16 (WS): Yo, p2tog, k3, p1, k3, p4, k3, p1, k4, k2tog.

Picking Sts up for Garter Stitch Edge

Insert rn tip into yo loop and k tbl.

PATTERN NOTES

Inspired by a carved stone found at the Great Mount of Knowth, the Knowth shawl is a semi-circular shawl knitted in two colours of Nua. Slipped stitches move across the garter-stitch surface until they are broken up by a contrast colour band decorated by a lacy cable. A garter-stitch ridge in the main colour finishes off the warm and practical shawl.

The shawl is semi-circular with the body formed by seven full wedges and two half-wedges (one each edge). Stitch markers are used to guide the knitter. Slip markers unless instructed otherwise. Markers A mark the edges; markers B mark increase points; markers C indicate slipped stitches.

An applied edge is worked perpendicular to the garter stitch and slipped stitch body. Stitches are then picked up along the applied edge and garter stitch is worked until shawl is bound off.

Edge Chart

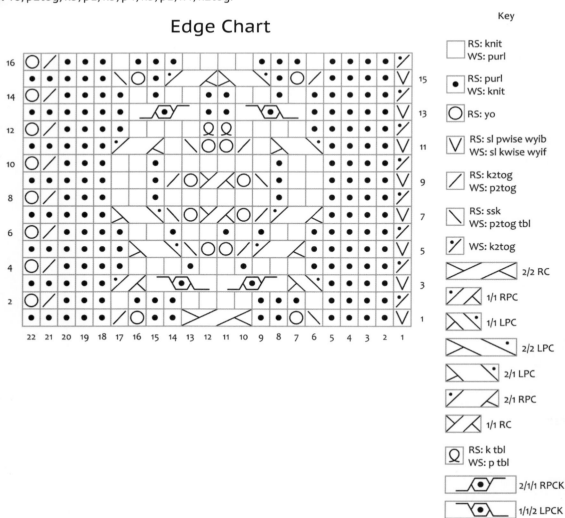

22

PATTERN

Garter Stitch Tab

Using MC, CO 2 sts.
Knit 8 rows.
Turn strip 90 degrees, pick up 1 st from each of the garter stitch bumps along the edge, then 2 sts from cast-on edge. *8 sts.*

Set-up

Row 1 (RS): K2, [kfb] 4 times, k2. *12 sts.*
Rows 2-4: Knit.
Row 5 (RS): K2, M1, [k1, M1] 8 times, k2. *21 sts.*
Row 6: Knit.

Begin Slip-stitch Pattern

Row 7 (RS): K2, *k1, M1; rep from * to last 3 sts, k3. *37 sts.*
Row 8 (WS): K3, *k1, sl1 wyif, k2; rep from * to last 2 sts, k2.
Row 9 (RS): Knit.
Rows 10 - 13: Rep Rows 8 - 9 twice.
Row 14 (WS): Rep row 8.

Row 15 (RS): K2, *k1, M1, k3, M1; rep from * to last 3 sts, k3. *53 sts.*
Row 16 (WS): K3, *k2, sl1 wyif, k3; rep from * to last 2 sts, k2.
Row 17 (RS): Knit.
Rows 18 - 21: Rep Rows 16 - 17 twice.
Row 22 (WS): Rep Row 16.
Row 23 (RS, placing markers A and B): K2, pm A *k1, M1L, k5, M1R, pm B; rep from * 6 more times, k1, M1L, k5, M1R, pm A, k3. *69 sts.*
Row 24 (WS, placing markers C): K3, *k3, sl1 wyif, pm C directly on the sl st, k4; rep from * 7 more times, k2.
Row 25 (RS): Knit.
Row 26 (WS): K3, sl m A, *knit to marker C, sl1 wyif; rep from * 7 more times, knit to end.
Rows 27 - 30: Rep Rows 25 – 26 twice.

Establish Pattern

Row 31 (RS): K2, sl m A, *k1, M1, knit to marker B, M1, sl m B; rep from * 6 more times, k1, M1, knit to marker A, M1, sl m A, k3. *85 sts.*
Row 32 (WS): K3, sl m A, *knit to marker C, sl1 wyif; rep from * 7 more times, knit to end.

Row 33 (RS): Knit.
Rows 34 - 37: Rep Rows 32 - 33 twice.
Row 38 (WS): Rep Row 32.

Rows 39-142: Rep Rows 31-38 another 13 times, increasing by 16 sts every 8th row. *293 sts.*

Join and work the next two rows with CC.
Row 143 (RS): K2, sl m A, *k1, M1, knit to marker C, sl1 wyib, knit to marker B, M1, sl m B rep from * 6 more times, k1, M1, knit to marker C, sl1 wyib, knit to marker A, M1, sl m A, k3. *309 sts.*
Row 144 (WS): K3, sl m A, *knit to marker C, sl1 wyif; rep from * 7 more times, knit to end.

Continue in MC.

Row 145 (RS): Knit.
Row 146 (WS): K3, sl m A, *knit to marker C, sl1 wyif; rep from * 7 more times, knit to end.
Row 147 (RS): K2, sl m A, *k1, M1, knit to marker B, M1, sl m B; rep from * 6 more times, k1, M1, knit to marker A, M1, sl m A, k3. *325 sts.*
Row 148 (WS): K3, sl m A, *knit to marker C, sl1 wyif; rep from * 7 more times, knit to end.

Change to CC.

Row 149 (RS): K2, sl m A, *knit to marker C, sl1 wyib; rep from * 7 more times, knit to end.
Row 150 (WS): K3, sl m A, *knit to marker C, sl1 wyif; rep from * 7 more times, knit to end.

Cut CC and continue working in MC, removing all markers as you work.

Rows 151 - 155: Knit.

With WS facing, cut MC.

Applied Edge

Join CC and CO 22 sts using the Knitted Cast-On method. Do not turn.

Set-up Row (WS): K21, k2tog with first st from shawl body. Turn work.
Next Row (RS): Knit. Turn work.
Next Rows (WS): K21, k2tog with first st from shawl body. Turn Work

Rep Edge Chart (or Written Directions) 40 times across shawl body sts. Note that on each WS row the final st in the applied edge will be worked together with the first st from the shawl body. After working the final rep, 3 shawl body sts and 22 edge sts rem.

Next Row (RS): Knit. Turn work.
Next Row (WS): K21, k2tog with first st from shawl body. Turn work.
Next Row (RS): Knit. Turn work.
Next Row (WS): K21, k2tog with first st from shawl body. Turn work.

Rep last two rows once more.

BO all sts.

Garter Stitch Edge

With RS facing and using MC, pick up and knit 341 sts along the Applied Edge.

Knit 6 rows.

With WS facing, BO as follows: k2, *put both sts back on onto ln, k2tog tbl, k1; rep from * to end.

FINISHING

Weave in ends. Block to size.

Epona

by Carol Feller

SIZES

One Size

FINISHED MEASUREMENTS

Circumference: 50.5" / 128.5 cm
Depth: 5.5" / 14 cm (11.25" / 28.5 cm circumference of tube)

YARN

Stolen Stitches 'Nua' (60% Merino, 20% Yak, 20% Linen, 153 yds / 140 m per 1.76 oz / 50 g); **Colours: C1:** Frog On the Wall (9802), 3 skeins; **C2:** Capall (9805), 1 skein; **C3:** Mosquito Coast (9801), 1 skein;
Approx Yardage Used: C1: 454 yds / 416 m; **C2/C3:** 148 yds / 135 m

NEEDLES & NOTIONS

US size 5 / 3.75 mm dpns
Second needle same size or smaller for grafting

Always use a needle size that gives you the gauge listed, as every knitter's gauge is unique.

Tapestry needle, stitch markers, waste yarn, US size 'e' / 3.5 mm crochet hook

GAUGE

29 sts and 27 rows = 4" / 10 cm in Stranded Colourwork blocked

ABBREVIATIONS

See Abbreviations Section on Page 74.

TECHNIQUES & STITCH PATTERNS

See Techniques Section on Page 75 for any additional techniques not detailed in pattern.

Spiral Chart

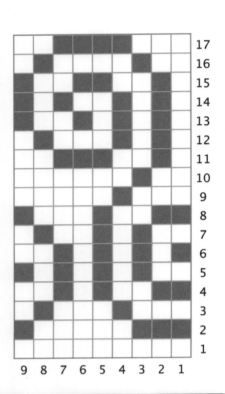

PATTERN NOTES

This cowl is exactly what you need for colder weather. The thick double layer combined with enough length to double up keeps you warm and looking great! The cowl is knit from side-to-side; it starts with a Provisional Cast-On and you then work in the round for the full length and graft the start and end together. This creates a double thickness cowl with patterning on both sides.

When working stranded colourwork you need to consistently keep one colour on each side (or above the other one). In this pattern C1 is is the background colour so it should remain in your right hand (or above the other colour). C2 and C3 are the pattern colour so they should stay in the left hand (or below the other colour). This allows C2/C3 to be dominant and stand out in the work.

PATTERN

Using Provisional Cast-On and waste yarn, CO 81 sts.
With C1, knit 1 row (Row 1 of Spiral Chart). Pm for start of rnd, join to work in rnd.
Set-Up Rnd: Reading Spiral Chart from right to left, using C1 and C2, starting on Rnd 2 of Spiral Chart, work 9 st patt rep 9 times.
Continue to work in patt as est'd until all 17 Rnds of Spiral Chart have been completed.
Work Rnds 1-17 of the Spiral Chart once more substituting C3 for C2.

Continue to work these 34 rnds as est'd 9 more times.
Work should measure approx 50.5" / 128.5 cm from cast-on.

FINISHING

Break yarns, leaving a tail 3-4 times the length of your rnd in C1. Undo Provisional Cast-On and place resultant sts on second needle.

Note: You will have to pick up an edge st to ensure you have the same number of sts on both sides.

Graft start and end of cowl together.
Weave in all loose ends.
Block cowl to dimensions given.

Trittico

by Woolly Wormhead

SIZES

Small (Large)
To Fit Head Circumference Up To: 20.75 (22.75)" / 52.5 (58) cm
4 - 5" / 10 – 12.5 cm negative ease recommended.

FINISHED MEASUREMENTS

Brim Circumference: 15.75 (17.75)" / 40 (45) cm
Depth: 7.75 (8.25)" / 19 (21) cm

YARN

Stolen Stitches 'Nua' (60% Merino, 20% Yak, 20% Linen, 153 yds / 140 m per 50 g); **Colour:** Hatter's Teal Party (9803), 1 (2) skeins;
Approx Yardage Used: 139 (169) yds / 127 (154) m

NEEDLES & NOTIONS

US 2.5 / 3 mm straight needles

Always use a needle size that gives you the gauge listed, as every knitter's gauge is unique.

3.5 mm crochet hook, 3 m waste yarn, tapestry needle, 2 cable needles

GAUGE

24 sts and 48 rows = 4" / 10 cm in Garter Stitch blocked

ABBREVIATIONS

See Abbreviations Section on Page 74.

TECHNIQUES & STITCH PATTERNS

See Techniques Section on Page 75 for any additional techniques not detailed in pattern.

SR

Work short row. For w&t method this is the stitch that is wrapped; for German Short Row method this is the double-legged stitch.

1/1 LC

Sl next st onto cn & hold at front of work, knit next st then knit the st from the cn (left twist).

1/1 RC

Sl next st onto cn & hold at back of work, knit next st then knit the st from the cn (right twist).

1/1/1 RC

Sl next stitch onto first cn and hold at back of work; slip next st onto second cn and hold at front of work; knit next st then knit the st held on the cn at the front, then finally knit the st from the cn at the back.

Key

- ☐ RS: knit
- ● WS: knit
- C SR
- V WS: sl st pwise wyif
- ⧄ 1/1 RC
- ⧅ 1/1 LC
- ⧄⧅ 1/1/1 RC
- ▨ Large Size Only
- ⌒ Bind Off
- O Pick Up St

Panel 1 Chart

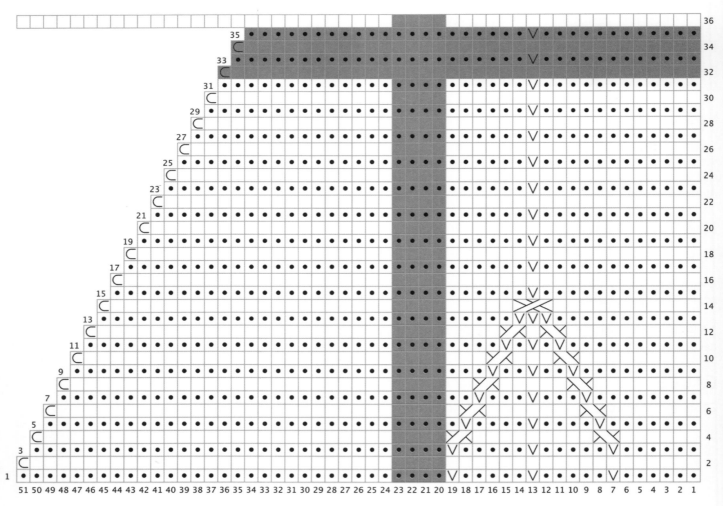

Panel 2 Chart

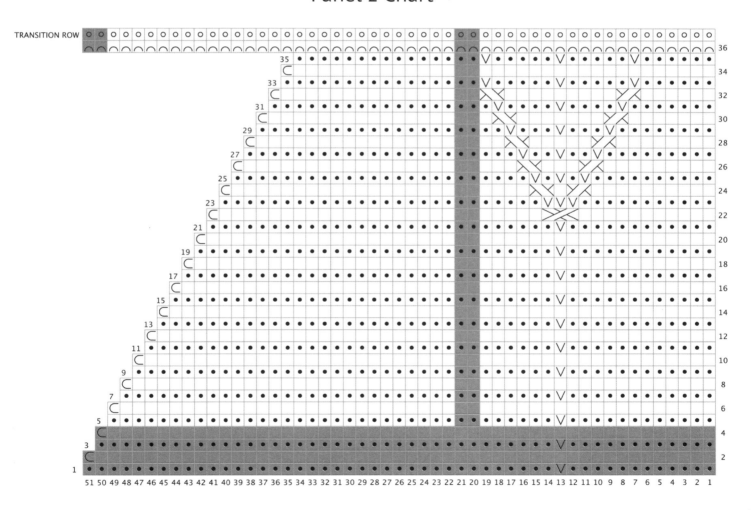

PATTERN NOTES

This hat is worked sideways as a series of panels; 6 panels in total. Two panels are worked consecutively then cast-off. Stitches are then picked up and the next two panels are worked. The process is repeated once more. Finally, the first and last panel are grafted together.

Row gauge determines the circumference, and stitch gauge determines the depth.

All slipped stitches are worked with yarn at front of work.

The hat is worn with a reasonable amount of negative ease, as garter stitch is particularly stretchy when worn sideways.

PATTERN

Using waste yarn and Crochet Provisional Cast-On, CO 47 (51) sts.

Switch to main yarn.

Panel 1

Row 1 (WS): K28 (32), [sl 1, k5] twice, sl1, k6.
Row 2 (RS): Knit to last st, SR.
Row 3 (WS): K27 (31), [sl1, k5] twice, sl1, k6.
Row 4 (RS): K6, 1/1 LC, k9, 1/1 RC, knit to st before last short rowed st, SR.
Row 5 (WS): K27 (31), [sl 1, k4] twice, sl 1, k7.
Row 6 (RS): K7, 1/1 LC, k7, 1/1 RC, knit to st before last short rowed st, SR.
Row 7 (WS): K27 (31), [sl 1, k3] twice, sl1, k8.
Row 8 (RS): K8, 1/1 LC, k5, 1/1 RC, knit to st before last short rowed st, SR.
Row 9 (WS): K27 (31), [sl 1, k2] twice, sl 1, k9.
Row 10 (RS): K9, 1/1 LC, k3, 1/1 RC, knit to st before last short rowed st, SR.
Row 11 (WS): K27 (31), [sl 1, k1] twice, sl 1, k10.
Row 12 (RS): K10, 1/1 LC, k1, 1/1 RC, knit to st before last short rowed st, SR.
Row 13 (WS): K27 (31), sl 3, k11.
Row 14 (RS): K11, 1/1/1 RC, knit to st before last short rowed st, SR.
Row 15 (WS): Knit to last 13 sts; sl 1, knit to end.
Row 16 (RS): Knit to st before last short rowed st, SR.
Row 17 (WS): Knit to last 13 sts; sl 1, knit to end.

Rows 18-31 (35): Rep Rows 16 & 17, 7 (9) more times until there are a total of 15 (17) short rowed sts on the left hand needle.

Row 32 (36) (RS): Knit across all sts, working previous short rowed sts as you go. Proceed to Panel 2.

Panel 2

Row 1 (WS): Knit to last 13 sts; sl 1, knit to end.
Row 2 (RS): Knit to last stitch, SR.
Row 3 (WS): Knit to last 13 sts; sl 1, knit to end.

Rows 4 – 17 (21): Rep Rows 2 & 3, 7 (9) more times until there are a total of 8 (10) short rowed sts on the left hand needle.

Row 18 (22) (RS): K11, 1/1/1 RC, knit to st before last short rowed st, SR.
Row 19 (23) (WS): K24 (26), sl 3, k11.
Row 20 (24) (RS): K10, 1/1 RC, k1, 1/1 LC, knit to st before last short rowed st, SR.
Row 21 (25) (WS): K22 (24), [sl 1, k1] twice, sl 1, k10.
Row 22 (26) (RS): K9, 1/1 RC, k3, 1/1 LC, knit to st before last short rowed st, SR.
Row 23 (27) (WS): K20 (22), [sl 1, k2] twice, sl 1, k9.
Row 24 (28) (RS): K8, 1/1 RC, k5, 1/1 LC, knit to st before last short rowed st, SR.
Row 25 (29) (WS): K18 (20), [sl 1, k3] twice, sl 1, k8.
Row 26 (30) (RS): K7, 1/1 RC, k7, 1/1 LC, knit to st before last short rowed st, SR.
Row 27 (31) (WS): K16 (18), [sl 1, k4] twice, sl 1, k7.
Row 28 (32) (RS): K6, 1/1 RC, k 9, 1/1 LC, knit to st before last short rowed st, SR.
Row 29 (33) (WS): K14 (16), [sl 1, k5] twice, sl 1, k6.
Row 30 (34) (RS): Knit to st before last short rowed st, SR.
Row 31 (35) (WS): K13 (15), [sl 1, k5] twice, sl 1, k6.
Row 32 (36) (RS): BO all sts, working previous short rowed sts as you go. Break yarn.

Transition Row: Pick up one stitch on the reverse of the cast-off chain for each stitch cast off. Do this by inserting the tip of your needle into the purl bump on the wrong side of the work.

Rejoin yarn to the narrow (crown) end of work before repeating Panels 1 and 2 twice more (6 panels in total).

FINISHING

Carefully remove the provisional cast-on, stitch by stitch. Ensure the stitch orientation is correct before starting the graft.

Most of the graft will be garter stitch; however to get the most invisible join, you'll want to graft the slipped stitches as smoothly as possible.

When you release the slipped stitches from the Provisional Cast-On, drop the wide loop that appears to sit across the slipped stitch and instead pick up each leg of the 'V' that sits below it. To ensure the graft works correctly, the right hand leg of the 'V' (with RS of the work facing) needs to be twisted inwards/to the left. It is recommended to place the released stitches on the back needle.

1. Work as per the garter stitch graft until you reach the point where you have two stitches on the front needle before the slipped stitch, and one stitch on the back needle before the slipped stitch legs. (Remembering that the back needle, which contains the released stitches, will have one fewer stitch in the garter section, and two legs in place of the slipped stitch)

2. Stitch 1, front needle – insert the needle knitwise, pull the yarn through then slip the stitch off the needle.

3. Stitch 2, front needle – insert the needle purlwise, pull the yarn through but leave the stitch on the needle.

4. Stitch 3, back needle – insert the needle knitwise, pull the yarn through then slip the stitch off the needle.

5. Stitch 4, back needle – insert the needle knitwise, pull the yarn through but leave the stitch on the needle.

6. Stitch 5, front needle – insert the needle purlwise, pull the yarn through then slip the stitch off the needle.

7. Stitch 6, front needle – insert the needle purlwise, pull the yarn through but leave the stitch on the needle.

8. Stitch 7, back needle – insert the needle purlwise, pull the yarn through then slip the stitch off the needle.

9. Stitch 8, back needle – insert the needle knitwise, pull the yarn through but leave the stitch on the needle.

10. After working the combined graft for the slipped stitches, continue working a garter stitch graft until you meet the next slipped stitch point, as indicated above. Repeat the process until all stitches have been grafted.

Shamrock

by Justyna Lorkowska

SIZES

XS (S, M, L, XL, 2XL, 3XL)
To Fit Bust Circumference Up To: 30 (34, 38, 42, 46, 50, 56)" /
76 (86, 96.5, 106.5, 117, 127, 142) cm
6 - 8" / 15 - 20 cm positive ease recommended.

FINISHED MEASUREMENTS

Finished Bust Circumference: 36.75 (41.5, 44.75, 48.75, 53.5,
57.5, 62.75)" / 92 (103.5, 112, 122, 133.5, 143.5, 157) cm
Size S modelled with 6.5" / 16.5 cm of positive ease.
Length from Back of Neck: 24.5 (24.75, 25.25, 25.75, 29.25, 30,
30.5)" / 62 (62.75, 64.5, 65, 74, 76, 77.5) cm

YARN

Stolen Stitches 'Nua' (60% Merino, 20% Linen, 20% Yak, 153
yds / 140 m per 1.76 oz. / 50g); **Colour:** Mosquito Coast (9801),
8 (9, 10, 11, 13, 14, 16) skeins;
Approx Yardage Used: 1160 (1305, 1445, 1575, 1910, 2090,
2380) yds / 1065 (1190, 1320, 1445, 1745, 1910, 2170) m

NEEDLES & NOTIONS

US size 6 / 4.0 mm circular needle, 32" / 80 cm long and dpns
(main needle)
US size 7 / 4.5 mm circular needle, 24" / 60 cm long or dpns
US size 8 / 5 mm circular needle, 24" / 60 cm long or dpns
US size 5 / 3.75 mm circular needle, 32" / 80 cm long
US size 4 / 3.5 mm circular needle, 32" / 80 cm long or dpns

*Always use a needle size that gives you the gauge listed, as every
knitter's gauge is unique.*

Stitch markers, 2 stitch holders or waste yarn, cable needle,
tapestry needle

GAUGE

18 sts and 36 rows = 3" x 5.25" / 7.5 cm x 13.5 cm in Diamond
Network Pattern (one patt rep) blocked using main needle
23 sts and 28 rows = 4" / 10 cm in St St blocked using main
needle

ABBREVIATIONS

See Abbreviations Section on Page 74.

TECHNIQUES & STITCH PATTERNS

See Techniques Section on Page 75 for any additional
techniques not detailed in pattern.

1/1 LC

Sl 1 st to cn, hold in front, k1, then k1 from cn.

1/1 LPC

Sl 1 st to cn, hold in front, p1, then k1 from cn.

1/1 RC

Sl 1 st to cn, hold in back, k1, then k1 from cn.

1/1 RPC

Sl 1 st to cn, hold in back, k1, then p1 from cn.

1x1 Rib (flat)

Row 1 (RS): *K1, p1; rep from * as directed.
All subsequent Rows: Knit the knits, purl the purls.

1x1 Rib (in the round)

Worked over an even number of sts.
All Rnds: *K1, p1; rep from * around.

Diamond Network Pattern

Note: Work chart in the round until Front/Back are divided at armholes. Then work chart back and forth in rows.

Use either Charted or Written Directions.

Sizes XS, S, L and XL (Written)

Set-up Rnd: P2, k2, *k4, p4, k2, p4, k4; rep from * to last 4 sts, k2, p2.

Rnd/Row 1 (RS): P2, k2, *k2, [1/1 RC, p4] twice, 1/1 RC, k2; rep from * to last 4 sts, k2, p2.

All even numbered Rnds or all WS Rows: Knit the knits and purl the purls.

Rnd/Row 3 (RS): P2, k2, *k1, 1/1 RPC, 1/1 LPC, p2, 1/1 RC, 1/1 LC, p2, 1/1 RPC, 1/1 LPC, k1; rep from * to last 4 sts, k2, p2.

Rnd/Row 5 (RS): P2, 1/1 LPC, *1/1 RPC, p2, 1/1 LPC, 1/1 RC, k2, 1/1 LC, 1/1 RPC, p2, 1/1 LPC; rep from * to last 4 sts, 1/1 RPC, p2.

Rnd/Row 7 (RS): P3, *1/1 LC, p4, 1/1 LC, k4, 1/1 LC, p4; rep from * to last 5 sts, 1/1 LC, p3.

Rnd/Row 9 (RS): P3, k1, *k1, p3, 1/1 RC, 1/1 LC, k2, 1/1 RC, 1/1 LC, p3, k1; rep from * to last 4 sts, k1, p3.

Rnd/Row 11 (RS): P3, *1/1 LC, p2, [1/1 RC, k2, 1/1 LC] twice, p2; rep from * to last 5 sts, 1/1 LC, p3.

Rnd/Row 13 (RS): P3, k1, *k1, p2, k5, 1/1 RC, k5, p2, k1; rep from * to last 4 sts, k1, p3.

Rnd/Row 15 (RS): P3, *1/1 LC, p2, 1/1 LPC, k2, 1/1 RC, 1/1 LC, k2, 1/1 RPC, p2; rep from * to last 5 sts, 1/1 LC, p3.

Rnd/Row 17 (RS): P3, k1, *k1, p3, 1/1 LPC, 1/1 RC, k2, 1/1 LC, 1/1 RPC, p3, k1; rep from * to last 4 sts, k1, p3.

Rnd/Row 19 (RS): Rep Rnd/Row 7.

Rnd/Row 21 (RS): P2, 1/1 RC, *1/1 LC, p2, 1/1 RPC, 1/1 LPC, k2, 1/1 RPC, 1/1 LPC, p2, 1/1 RC; rep from * to last 4 sts, 1/1 LC, p2.

Rnd/Row 23 (RS): P2, k2, *k1, 1/1 LC, [1/1 RPC, p2, 1/1 LPC] twice, 1/1 RC, k1; rep from * to last 4 sts, k2, p2.

Rnd/Row 25 (RS): Rep Rnd/Row 1.

Rnd/Row 27 (RS): P2, k2, *k1, 1/1 RC, 1/1 LC, p3, k2, p3, 1/1 RC, 1/1 LC, k1; rep from * to last 4 sts, k2, p2.

Rnd/Row 29 (RS): P2, 1/1 LC, *1/1 RC, k2, 1/1 LC, [p2, 1/1 RC] twice, k2, 1/1 LC; rep from * to last 4 sts, 1/1 RC, p2.

Rnd/Row 31 (RS): P2, k1, *1/1 LC, k5, p2, k2, p2, k5; rep from * to last 5 sts, 1/1 LC, k1, p2.

Rnd/Row 33 (RS): P2, 1/1 RC, *1/1 LC, k2, 1/1 RPC, p2, 1/1 RC, p2, 1/1 LPC, k2, 1/1 RC; rep from * to last 4 sts, 1/1 LC, p2.

Rnd/Row 35 (RS): P2, k2, *k1, 1/1 LC, 1/1 RPC, p3, k2, p3, 1/1 LPC, 1/1 RC, k1; rep from * to last 4 sts, k2, p2.

Rnd 36 (RS)/Row 36 (WS): Knit the knits and purl the purls.

Sizes XS, S, L and XL (Charted)

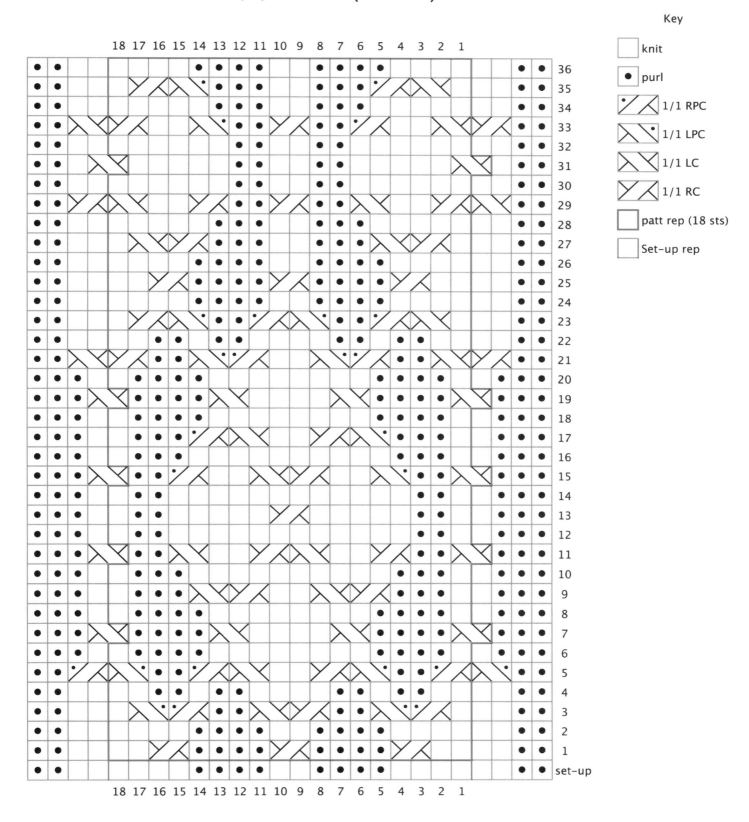

Key

☐	knit
●	purl
⟋	1/1 RPC
⟍	1/1 LPC
⟋	1/1 LC
⟍	1/1 RC
☐	patt rep (18 sts)
☐	Set-up rep

Sizes M, 2XL and 3XL (Charted)

Sizes M, 2XL and 3XL (Written)

Set-up Rnd: P5, k4, *k4, p4, k2, p4, k4; rep from * to last 9 sts, k4, p5.

Rnd 1/Row 1 (RS): P5, 1/1 RC, k2, *k2, [1/1 RC, p4] twice, 1/1 RC, k2; rep from * to last 9 sts, k2, 1/1 RC, p5.

All even numbered Rnds or all WS Rows: Knit the knits and purl the purls.

Rnd/Row 3 (RS): P4, 1/1 RPC, 1/1 LPC, k1, *k1, 1/1 RPC, 1/1 LPC, p2, 1/1 RC, 1/1 LC, p2, 1/1 RPC, 1/1 LPC, k1; rep from * to last 9 sts, k1, 1/1 RPC, 1/1 LPC, p4.

Rnd/Row 5 (RS): P3, 1/1 RPC, p2, 1/1 LPC, *1/1 RPC, p2, 1/1 LPC, 1/1 RC, k2, 1/1 LC, 1/1 RPC, p2, 1/1 LPC; rep from * to last 9 sts, 1/1 RPC, p2, 1/1 LPC, p3.

Rnd/Row 7 (RS): P2, 1/1 LC, p4, *1/1 LC, p4, 1/1 LC, k4, 1/1 LC, p4; rep from * to last 10 sts, 1/1 LC, p4, 1/1 LC, p2.

Rnd/Row 9 (RS): P2, k1, 1/1 LC, p3, k1, *k1, p3, 1/1 RC, 1/1 LC, k2, 1/1 RC, 1/1 LC, p3, k1; rep from * to last 9 sts, k1, p3, 1/1 RC, k1, p2.

Rnd/Row 11 (RS): P2, k2, 1/1 LC, p2, *1/1 LC, p2, [1/1 RC, k2, 1/1 LC] twice, p2; rep from * to last 10 sts, 1/1 LC, p2, 1/1 RC, k2, p2.

Rnd/Row 13 (RS): P2, k4, p2, k1, *k1, p2, k5, 1/1 RC, k5, p2, k1; rep from * to last 9 sts, k1, p2, k4, p2.

Rnd/Row 15 (RS): P2, k2, 1/1 RPC, p2, *1/1 LC, p2, 1/1 LPC, k2, 1/1 RC, 1/1 LC, k2, 1/1 RPC, p2; rep from * to last 10 sts, 1/1 LC, p2, 1/1 LPC, k2, p2.

Rnd/Row 17 (RS): P2, k1, 1/1 RPC, p3, k1, *k1, p3, 1/1 LPC, 1/1 RC, k2, 1/1 LC, 1/1 RPC, p3, k1; rep from * to last 9 sts, k1, p3, 1/1 LPC, k1, p2.

Rnd/Row 19 (RS): P2, 1/1 LPC, p4, *1/1 LC, p4, 1/1 LC, k4, 1/1 LC, p4; rep from * to last 10 sts, 1/1 LC, p4, 1/1 RPC, p2.

Rnd/Row 21 (RS): P3, 1/1 LPC, p2, 1/1 RC, *1/1 LC, p2, 1/1 RPC, 1/1 LPC, k2, 1/1 RPC, 1/1 LPC, p2, 1/1 RC; rep from * to last 9 sts, 1/1 LC, p2, 1/1 RPC, p3.

Rnd/Row 23 (RS): P4, 1/1 LPC, 1/1 RC, k1, *k1, 1/1 LC, [1/1 RPC, p2, 1/1 LPC] twice, 1/1 RC, k1; rep from * to last 9 sts, k1, 1/1 LC, 1/1 RPC, p4.

Rnd/Row 25 (RS): Rep Rnd/Row 1.

Rnd/Row 27 (RS): P4, 1/1 RC, 1/1 LC, k1, *k1, 1/1 RC, 1/1 LC, p3, k2, p3, 1/1 RC, 1/1 LC, k1; rep from * to last 9 sts, k1, 1/1 RC, 1/1 LC, p4.

Rnd/Row 29 (RS): P3, 1/1 RC, k2, 1/1 LC, *1/1 RC, k2, 1/1 LC, p2, 1/1 RC, p2, 1/1 RC, k2, 1/1 LC; rep from * to last 9 sts, 1/1 RC, k2, 1/1 LC, p3.

Rnd/Row 31 (RS): P3, k5, *1/1 LC, k5, p2, k2, p2, k5; rep from * to last 10 sts, 1/1 LC, k5, p3.

Rnd/Row 33 (RS): P3, 1/1 LPC, k2, 1/1 RC, *1/1 LC, k2, 1/1 RPC, p2, 1/1 RC, p2, 1/1 LPC, k2, 1/1 RC; rep from * to last 9 sts, 1/1 LC, k2, 1/1 RPC, p3.

Rnd/Row 35 (RS): P4, 1/1 LPC, 1/1 RC, k1, *k1, 1/1 LC, 1/1 RPC, p3, k2, p3, 1/1 LPC, 1/1 RC, k1; rep from * to last 9 sts, k1, 1/1 LC, 1/1 RPC, p4.

Rnd 36 (RS)/Row 36 (WS): Knit the knits and purl the purls.

PATTERN NOTES

The pullover is worked seamlessly from the bottom up. The entire body is worked in Diamond Network pattern based on simple 1/1 cables. Front and back are divided at armholes and shaped separately then joined at the shoulders using a centred double decrease. Stitches are picked up around the neck which is then finished with a ribbed cowl neck using increasingly larger needles. Finally, the stockinette sleeves with ribbed cuffs are worked in the round.

PATTERN

Bottom Hem

Using preferred method and smallest size needles, US size 4 / 3.5 mm, CO 220 (248, 268, 292, 320, 344, 376) sts.
Join for working in the rnd making sure not to twist the sts and pm for beginning of rnd.
Work in 1x1 Rib for 2" / 5 cm.
In the final rnd of ribbing, place second marker after 110 (124, 134, 146, 160, 172, 188) sts to indicate opposite side.

Body

Change to main needles, US size 6 / 4.0 mm.
Set-up Rnd: *K6 (4, 4, 6, 4, 5, 4), work Diamond Network Chart set-up rnd to 6 (4, 4, 6, 4, 5, 4) sts before m, k6 (4, 4, 6, 4, 5, 4); rep from * once more.
Work Rnds 1-36 of Diamond Network Chart 2 (2, 2, 2, 3, 3, 3) times as est'd, then rep Rnds 1-32 (32, 32, 32, 14, 14, 14) once more.
104 (104, 104, 104, 122, 122, 122) rnds total.

Upper Front

Next Row (RS): BO 3 (2, 2, 2, 2, 3, 2) sts, work in patt to m, remove m, turn work.
Next Row (WS): BO 3 (2, 2, 2, 2, 3, 2) sts, work in patt to end.
104 (120, 130, 142, 156, 166, 184) Front sts ending with Chart Row 34 (34, 34, 34, 16, 16, 16).
Place Back sts on holder or waste yarn, or simply let them rest on needle.
Work back and forth in patt for 34 (36, 38, 40, 46, 50, 54) more rows ending with Chart Row 32 (34, 36, 2, 26, 30, 34).

Begin 1x1 Rib and Shape Neck

Change to smaller size needles, US size 5 / 3.75 mm.
Next Row (RS): K1, *k1, p1; rep from * 17 (19, 20, 21, 23, 25, 28) more times, k2, BO 26 (34, 40, 48, 54, 56, 62) sts, *k1, p1; rep from * to last 2 sts, k2.
39 (43, 45, 47, 51, 55, 61) sts each shoulder.

Shape Right Shoulder

Next Row (WS): Knit the knits, purl the purls.
Row 1 (Neck Dec) (RS): K1, ssk, work in patt to end. *1 st dec'd*
Row 2 (WS): Knit the knits, purl the purls.
Short Row 1 (RS): K1, ssk, work in patt to 6 (6, 6, 6, 8, 8, 10) sts before end, w&t. *1 st dec'd*
Short Row 2 (WS): Rep Row 2.
Short Row 3 (RS): K1, ssk, work in patt to 6 (6, 6, 6, 8, 8, 10) sts before previous wrapped st, w&t. *1 st dec'd*
Short Row 4 (WS): Rep Row 2.
Short Rows 5 & 6: Rep last 2 rows once more. *1 st dec'd*
Short Row 7 (RS): Work in patt to 6 (6, 6, 6, 8, 8, 10) sts before previous wrapped st, w&t.
Short Row 8 (WS): Rep Row 2.
35 (39, 41, 43, 47, 51, 57) sts for Right Front shoulder.

Work 2 (2, 4, 4, 4, 6, 6) rows in 1x1 Rib picking up each wrap and working them together with their wrapped sts.
Break yarn and move sts to stitch holder or waste yarn.

Shape Left Shoulder

Attach yarn on WS and continue with smaller size needles, US size 5 / 3.75 mm.
Next Row (WS): Knit the knits, purl the purls.
Row 1 (Neck Dec) (RS): Work in patt to last 3 sts, k2tog, k1. *1 st dec'd*
Row 2 (WS): Knit the knits, purl the purls.
Short Row 1 (RS): Rep Row 1. *1 st dec'd*
Short Row 2 (WS): Work in patt to 6 (6, 6, 6, 8, 8, 10) sts before end, w&t.
Short Row 3 (RS): Rep Row 1. *1 st dec'd*
Short Row 4 (WS): Work in patt to 6 (6, 6, 6, 8, 8, 10) sts before previous wrapped st, w&t.
Short Rows 5 & 6: Rep last 2 rows once more. *1 st dec'd*
Short Row 7 (RS): Work in patt to end.
Short Row 8 (WS): Rep Short Row 4.
35 (39, 41, 43, 47, 51, 57) sts for Left Front shoulder.
Work 2 (2, 4, 4, 4, 6, 6) rows in 1x1 Rib picking up each wrap and working them together with their wrapped sts. Break yarn and move sts to stitch holder or waste yarn.

Back

With RS facing attach yarn and continue with main needles, US size 6 / 4.0 mm.
Next Row (RS): BO 3 (2, 2, 2, 2, 3, 2) sts, work in patt to end resuming with Chart Row 33 (33, 33, 33, 15, 15, 15).
Next Row (WS): BO 3 (2, 2, 2, 2, 3, 2) sts, work in patt to end.
104 (120, 130, 142, 156, 166, 184) sts.
Work back and forth in patt for 34 (36, 38, 40, 46, 50, 54) more rows ending with Chart Row 32 (34, 36, 2, 26, 30, 34).

Change to smaller size needles, US size 5 / 3.75 mm.
Begin 1x1 Rib
Next Row (RS): K1, *k1, p1; rep from * to last 3 sts, k2tog, k1.
103 (119, 129, 141, 155, 165, 183) sts rem.
Next Row (WS): P2, *k1, p1; rep from * to last st, p1.
Work 2 more rows in patt.

Shape Shoulders

Short Row 1 (RS): Work in patt to 6 (6, 6, 6, 8, 8, 10) sts before end, w&t.
Short Row 2 (WS): Work in patt to 6 (6, 6, 6, 8, 8, 10) sts before end, w&t.
Short Row 3 (RS): Work in patt to 6 (6, 6, 6, 8, 8, 10) sts before previous wrapped st, w&t.
Short Row 4 (WS): Work in patt to 6 (6, 6, 6, 8, 8, 10) sts before previous wrapped st, w&t.
Rep last 2 rows twice more.
Work 2 (2, 4, 4, 4, 6, 6) rows to end in 1x1 Rib picking up each wrap and working them together with their wrapped sts.
Break yarn.

Join Shoulders

Front and back shoulders are joined with a Centred Double Decrease, with the middle of the decrease forming the seam. Place Right Front sts on main needle, US size 6 / 4.0 mm. With RS facing hold Right Front shoulder on right needle and Back on left needle with needle tips facing each other.
Sl 1 st from right needle to left needle, attach new yarn and work k2tog.
*Sl 2 sts from right needle to left needle then slip them together knitwise back to the right needle, k1 and p2sso; rep from * until you BO all Right Shoulder sts, fasten off final st. Break yarn.
Place Left Front sts on main needle, US size 6 / 4.0 mm. With RS racing hold Back on right needle and Left Front on left needle with needle tips facing each other. Join shoulder seam as for Right Shoulder.
Break yarn.
Both shoulders are seamed and 33 (41, 47, 55, 61, 63, 69) live back neck sts remain on the needle.

Cowl Neck

With US size 5 / 3.75 mm needles and starting at left shoulder, pick up an odd number of sts along left shoulder, front neck, right shoulder (approx 4 sts for every 5 rows), then work across back neck sts. Total number of sts must be even. Join for working in the rnd and pm for beginning of rnd.
Work in 1X1 Rib for 4" / 10 cm then change to main needle, US size 6 / 4.0 mm. *Continue in patt for 2"/ 5 cm more then change to next larger needle. Rep from * once more then with largest needle work until cowl measures 9" / 22.5 cm.
BO all sts in patt loosely or using a stretchy BO method.

Sleeves

Attach yarn at underarm and using main needle, US size 6 / 4.0 mm, pick up 60 (64, 70, 76, 82, 88, 94) sts around the armhole, equally divided before and after the top-of-shoulder seam.
Knit three rnds.
Short Row 1 (RS): K40 (42, 45, 48, 51, 54, 57), w&t.
Short Row 2 (WS): P20, w&t.
Short Row 3 (RS): Knit to wrapped st, pick up wrap and work together with wrapped st, k10, w&t.
Short Row 4 (WS): Purl to wrapped st, pick up wrap and work together with wrapped st, p10, w&t.
Next Row (RS): Knit to m, picking up the wrap and working it together with its wrapped st.
Next Rnd: Knit around, picking up the final wrap.
Knit three rnds even.
Dec Rnd: K1, k2tog, knit to last 3 sts, ssk, k1. *2 sts dec'd*
Rep Dec Rnd every 14th (14th, 12th, 10th, 8th, 6th, 6th) rnd 5 (5, 6, 8, 8, 10, 11) more times.
48 (52, 56, 58, 64, 66, 70) sts.
Work even in St St until sleeve measures 15" / 38 cm or 2" / 5 cm less than desired length.
Change to smallest needles US size 4 / 3.5 mm, and work in 1x1 Rib in the rnd until cuff measures 2" / 5 cm.
BO all sts in patt in the next rnd.
Rep for other sleeve.

FINISHING

Weave in ends then block to measurements.

SCHEMATIC

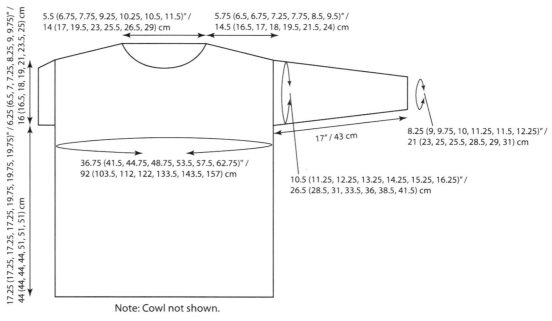

5.5 (6.75, 7.75, 9.25, 10.25, 10.5, 11.5)" / 14 (17, 19.5, 23, 25.5, 26.5, 29) cm

5.75 (6.5, 6.75, 7.25, 7.75, 8.5, 9.5)" / 14.5 (16.5, 17, 18, 19.5, 21.5, 24) cm

6.25 (6.5, 7, 7.25, 8.25, 9, 9.75)" / 16 (16.5, 18, 19, 21, 23.5, 25) cm

17.25 (17.25, 17.25, 17.25, 19.75, 19.75, 19.75)" / 44 (44, 44, 44, 51, 51, 51) cm

8.25 (9, 9.75, 10, 11.25, 11.5, 12.25)" / 21 (23, 25, 25.5, 28.5, 29, 31) cm

17" / 43 cm

36.75 (41.5, 44.75, 48.75, 53.5, 57.5, 62.75)" / 92 (103.5, 112, 122, 133.5, 143.5, 157) cm

10.5 (11.25, 12.25, 13.25, 14.25, 15.25, 16.25)" / 26.5 (28.5, 31, 33.5, 36, 38.5, 41.5) cm

Note: Cowl not shown.

Ahenny

by Jennifer Wood

SIZES

To Fit Bust Size Up To: 33.25 (36, 38.25, 41.25, 44.5, 47.75, 49.75, 52.5, 54.5)" / 84.5 (91.5, 97, 105, 113, 121.5, 126.5, 133.5, 138.5) cm
0 - 2" / 0 - 5 cm negative ease recommended.

FINISHED MEASUREMENTS

Finished Bust Circumference: 31.25 (34, 36.25, 39.25, 42.5, 45.75, 47.75, 50.5, 52.5)" / 79.5 (86.5, 92, 99.5, 108, 116, 121.5, 128.5, 133.5) cm
Note: These dimensions are from below front cable.
Size 34" / 86.5 modelled with no ease.
Length from Back of Neck: 20.5 (21.5, 23.25, 23.75, 24.75, 24.75, 26.25, 26.5, 27.25)" / 52.25 (54.5, 59, 60, 63, 63, 67, 67.5, 69) cm

YARN

Stolen Stitches 'Nua' (60% Merino, 20% Yak, 20% Linen, 153 yds/140 m per 1.76 oz / 50g); **Colour:** Bare Necessities (9806), 5 (6, 7, 7, 8, 9, 10, 10, 12) skeins;
Approx Yardage Used: 755 (840, 965, 1065, 1190, 1275, 1390, 1490, 1695) yds / 695 (770, 880, 975, 1085, 1165, 1275, 1365, 1550) m

NEEDLES & NOTIONS

US size 3 / 3.25 mm circular needles, 18" / 40cm long and 24"/ 60 cm long (or longer for larger sizes)
US size 3 / 3.25 mm dpns

Always use a needle size that gives you the gauge listed, as every knitter's gauge is unique.

Removable markers, tapestry needle, cable needle

GAUGE

22 sts and 28 rows = 4" / 10 cm in St St blocked
Front Cable meas 4.75" / 12 cm across
Back Cable meas 5.5" / 14 cm across
Sleeve Cable meas 3.25" / 8.5 cm across
Cable Chart meas 1" / 2.5 cm across

ABBREVIATIONS

See Abbreviations Section on Page 74.

TECHNIQUES & STITCH PATTERNS

See Techniques Section on Page 75 for any additional techniques not detailed in pattern.

Purl Rib

Multiple of 3 sts
Rnd 1: * P1, k1, p1, repeat from * to end.
Rnd 2: * K1, p2, repeat from * to end.

Charts

Use either written or charted directions. All written directions for these charts are available in the electronic version of the book.

Key

☐ knit

• purl

▣ no stitch

Ⓞ M1

Ⓞ M1p

1/1 RC: Sl 1 st to cn, hold to back, k1, k1 from cn

1/1 LC: Sl 1 st to cn, hold to front, k1, k1 from cn

1/1 RPC: Sl 1 st to cn, hold to back, k1, p1 from cn

1/1 LPC: Sl 1 st to cn, hold to front, p1 from cn

2/1 RPC: Sl 1 st to cn, hold to back, k2, p1 from cn

2/1 LPC: Sl 2 sts to cn, hold to front, p1, k2 from cn

2/2 RC: Sl 2 sts to cn, hold to back, k2, k2 from cn

2/2 LC: Sl 2 sts to cn, hold to front, k2, k2 from cn

2/2 RPC: Sl 2 sts to cn, hold to back, k2, p2 from cn

2/2 LPC: Slip 2 sts to cn, hold to front, k2, p2 from cn

2/1/2 LPC: Slip 2 sts to cn, hold to front, k2, p1, k2 from cn

☐ patt repeat

◹ ssk

CABLE CHART

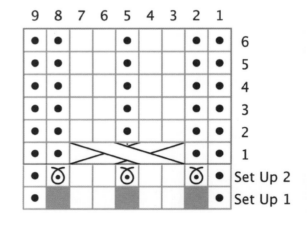

9	8	7	6	5	4	3	2	1	
•	•			•			•	•	6
•	•			•			•	•	5
•	•			•			•	•	4
•	•			•			•	•	3
•	•			•			•	•	2
•	•	╳	╳	╳	╳		•	•	1
•	Ⓞ			Ⓞ			Ⓞ	•	Set Up 2
•	▣			▣			▣	•	Set Up 1

SLEEVE CABLE CHART

FRONT CABLE CHART

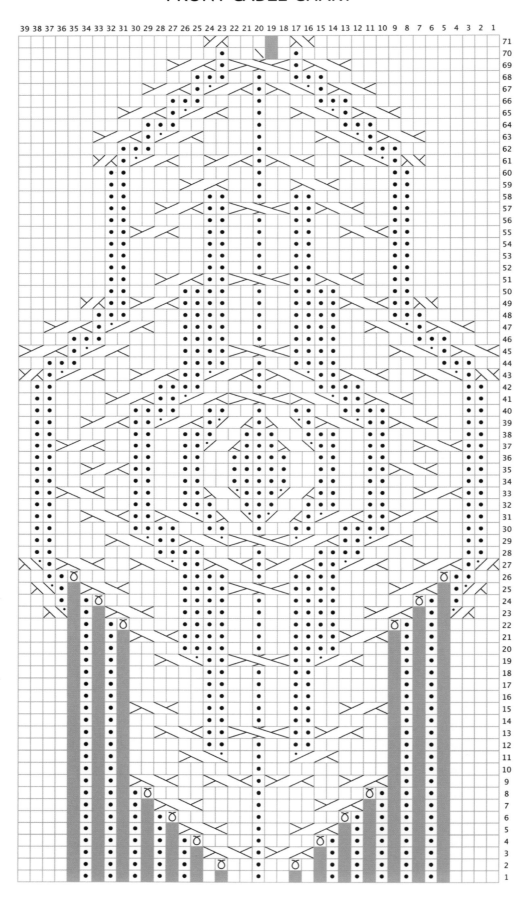

BACK CABLE CHART

PATTERN NOTES

This sweater starts as a rounded yoke and then moves into raglan constructed from the top down in one piece.

This pullover is designed with negative ease in the bust. If you desire a looser fit work one size bigger.

Sleeve and body length is easily adjusted.

PATTERN

Yoke

With shorter circ CO 131 (131, 135, 139, 141, 143, 143, 145, 145) sts. Place marker (pm) and join for working in the rnd, making sure the sts are not twisted.
Purl one rnd.

Note: The chart markers and the markers to divide the sleeve sts from the body stitches are placed in the next round. You may want to use a different color for the Cable Chart Markers (cm) and Raglan Markers (rm)

Change to a longer circ when needed to accommodate the increasing number of stitches.

Set-up Rnd: K2 (2, 3, 3, 3, 3, 3, 3, 3) for Left Sleeve, place cm for Sleeve Chart, work Rnd 1 of Sleeve Chart, place cm, k2 (2, 3, 3, 3, 3, 3, 3, 3), place rm, k3 (3, 3, 4, 4, 5, 5, 5, 5) for Back , place cm for Back Chart, work Rnd 1 of Back Chart, place cm, k3 (3, 3, 4, 4, 5, 5, 5, 5), place rm, k2 (2, 3, 3, 3, 3, 3, 3, 3) for Right Sleeve, place cm for Sleeve Chart, work Rnd 1 of Sleeve Chart, place cm, k2 (2, 3, 3, 3, 3, 3, 3, 3), place rm, k11 (11, 11, 12, 13, 13, 13, 14, 14) for Front, place cm, work Rnd 1 of Front Chart, place cm, k11 (11, 11, 12, 13, 13, 13, 14, 14), end of rnd m is final rm. *22 (22, 24, 24, 24, 24, 24, 24, 24) Sleeve sts, 40 (40, 40, 42, 42, 44, 44, 44, 44) Back sts, 47 (47, 47, 49, 51, 51, 51, 53, 53) Front sts.*

Next Rnd: Sl all m as you come to them, knit to Sleeve cm, work Rnd 2 of Sleeve Chart, knit to Back cm, work Rnd 2 of Back Chart, knit to Sleeve cm, work Rnd 2 of Sleeve Chart, knit to Front cm, work Rnd 2 of Front Chart, knit to end.
Work 6 more rnds in pattern as established working the chart rows sequentially between chart markers. *31 (31, 33, 33, 33, 33, 33, 33, 33) Sleeve sts, 55 (55, 55, 57, 57, 59, 59, 59, 59) Back sts, 55 (55, 55, 57, 59, 59, 59, 61, 61) Front sts.*

Note: Sizes - (-, 36.25, 39.25, 42.5, 45.75, 47.75, 50.5, 52.5)" / - (-, 92, 99.5, 108, 116, 121.5, 128.5, 133.5) cm when Sleeve Chart is completed switch to Cable Chart starting on Rnd 2.

Raglan Inc Rnd: [K1, RLI, work in patt to 1 st before next rm, LLI, k1, sl m] 4 times. *8 sts inc'd.*
Work one rnd even working the new sts in St St.
Rep these two rnds 9 (11, 14, 17, 18, 18, 21, 22, 22) more times.

Total Sts: *258 (274, 302, 330, 340, 342, 366, 376, 376); 51 (55, 63, 69, 71, 71, 77, 79, 79) Sleeve sts, 75 (79, 85, 93, 95, 97, 103, 105, 105), Back sts, 81 (85, 91, 99, 103, 103, 109, 113, 113) Front sts.*

Note: Sizes 31.25 (34)" / 79.5 (86.5) cm when Sleeve Chart is completed switch to Cable Chart starting on Rnd 2.

Body Inc Rnd: [Work across Sleeve sts, sl rm, k1, RLI, work in patt to 1 st before next rm, LLI, k1, sl m] twice. *4 sts inc'd.*
Work one rnd even in patt working the new sts in St St.
Rep these two rnds 3 (4, 5, 4, 4, 4, 5, 5, 7) more times.

Total Sts: *274 (294, 326, 350, 360, 362, 390, 400, 407); 51 (55, 63, 69, 71, 71, 77, 79, 79) Sleeve sts, 83 (89, 97, 103, 105, 107, 115, 117, 121) Back sts, 89 (95, 103, 109, 113, 113, 121, 125, 128) Front sts.*

Body

At this point, the sleeves and body will be divided.
The lower body will be worked first, then the sleeves.

Dividing Rnd: Remove rm, put Left Sleeve sts on holder, CO 2 (3, 2, 3, 6, 10, 9, 11, 12) sts, place cm for Cable Chart, this marker is the new beginning of rnd use unique colour, CO 6 sts, place cm, CO 2 (3, 2, 3, 6, 10, 9, 11, 12), work across Back sts to next Sleeve rm, remove rm, put Right Sleeve sts on holder, CO 2 (3, 2, 3, 6, 10, 9, 11, 12) sts, place cm for Cable Chart, CO 6 sts, place cm, CO 2 (3, 2, 3, 6, 10, 9, 11, 12) sts, remove rm, work to end. *192 (208, 220, 236, 254, 272, 284, 298, 309) Body sts.*

Next Rnd: Working the CO sts outside the Cable Chart markers in St St work in est'd patt to the Cable Chart cm, sl cm, work Set Up Rnd 1 of Cable Chart, sl cm, work to next cm, sl cm, work Set Up Rnd 1 of Cable Chart, sl cm, work to end.

Note: Continue working charts in patt as est'd while working the Front Decs & Back Incs as described below. After Set Up Rnd 2 has been worked on the Cable Chart rep Rnds 1 – 6 for patt. Once the Front Chart is completed, remove cm, and work all Front sts in St St.

Note: After Cable Chart Set-Up 3 sts are added to each side. After Front Chart is complete 1 st is dec'd. 197 (213, 225, 241, 259, 277, 289, 303, 315) sts.

Inc/Dec Rnd: Work Cable Chart, sl cm, k1, RLI, work across Back sts to 1 st before next Cable Chart cm, LLI, k1, sl cm, work Cable Chart, sl cm, k1, ssk, work to 3 sts before end of rnd, k2tog, k1, sl cm. Work 3 (3, 3, 3, 4, 4, 5, 5, 5) rnds even in patt. Rep these 4 (4, 4, 4, 5, 5, 6, 6, 6) rnds 23 (23, 24, 24, 20, 20, 17, 17, 17) more times.

Purl Rib Band

Note: You need a multiple of 3 for the Purl Rib.

Dec Rnd: Removing cms as you go, p2, k2tog, p1, k2tog, p2, remove cm, knit to Back Chart cm, remove cm, k5 [k2tog] 19 times, k5, remove cm, knit to Cable Chart cm, p2, k2tog, p1, k2tog, p2, knit to end decreasing 0 (1, 1, 2, 2, 2, 2, 1, 1) sts. *174 (189, 201, 216, 234, 252, 264, 279, 291) sts.*

Work Purl Rib for 9 rnds or desired length. BO in pattern.

Sleeves

Use your preferred needle type for working small circumferences; long circ for magic loop, dpns or 2 circ.

With dpns, RS facing, and beg at center of underarm, pick up and knit 5 (6, 5, 6, 9, 13, 12, 14, 15) sts along CO sts, work 51 (55, 63, 69, 71, 71, 77, 79, 79) held Sleeve sts, pick up and knit 5 (6, 5, 6, 9, 13, 12, 14, 15) sts along CO sts to center of underarm, pm and join in the rnd. *61 (67, 73, 81, 89, 97, 101, 107, 109) sts.*

Work 11 (8, 6, 5, 4, 3, 3, 3, 2) rnds working the Cable Chart between cms.

Dec Rnd: K1, k2tog, work in patt to last 2 sts, ssk. *2 sts dec'd.*
Rep these 12 (9, 7, 6, 5, 4, 4, 4, 3) rnds 6 (9, 12, 13, 17, 18, 20, 23, 24) more times. *47 (47, 47, 53, 53, 59, 59, 59, 59) sts.*

Work 5 (1, 1, 8, 4, 18, 10, 0, 21) more rnd(s) even in patt.

Cuff

Note: *You need a multiple of 3 for the Purl Rib.*

Set Up Rnd: Removing cms as you go, knit to cm, p2, k2tog, p1, k2tog, p2, knit to end. *45 (45, 45, 51, 51, 57, 57, 57, 57) sts.* Work Purl Rib Stitch for 6 rnds or desired length. BO in pattern.

FINISHING

Wet block and weave loose ends.

SCHEMATIC

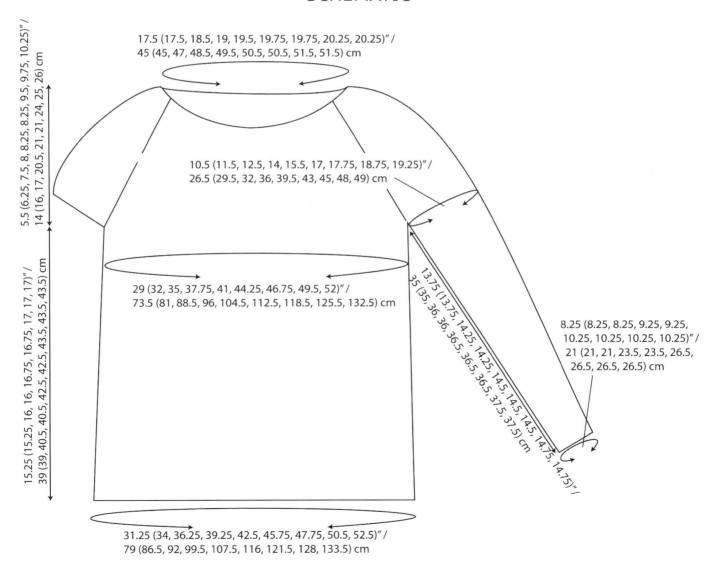

17.5 (17.5, 18.5, 19, 19.5, 19.75, 19.75, 20.25, 20.25)" / 45 (45, 47, 48.5, 49.5, 50.5, 50.5, 51.5, 51.5) cm

5.5 (6.25, 7.5, 8, 8.25, 8.25, 9.5, 9.75, 10.25)" / 14 (16, 17, 20.5, 21, 21, 24, 25, 26) cm

10.5 (11.5, 12.5, 14, 15.5, 17, 17.75, 18.75, 19.25)" / 26.5 (29.5, 32, 36, 39.5, 43, 45, 48, 49) cm

15.25 (15.25, 16, 16, 16.75, 16.75, 17, 17, 17)" / 39 (39, 40.5, 40.5, 42.5, 42.5, 43.5, 43.5, 43.5) cm

29 (32, 35, 37.75, 41, 44.25, 46.75, 49.5, 52)" / 73.5 (81, 88.5, 96, 104.5, 112.5, 118.5, 125.5, 132.5) cm

13.75 (13.75, 14.25, 14.25, 14.5, 14.5, 14.5, 14.75, 14.75)" / 35 (35, 36, 36.5, 36.5, 36.5, 37.5, 37.5) cm

8.25 (8.25, 8.25, 9.25, 9.25, 10.25, 10.25, 10.25, 10.25)" / 21 (21, 21, 23.5, 23.5, 26.5, 26.5, 26.5, 26.5) cm

31.25 (34, 36.25, 39.25, 42.5, 45.75, 47.75, 50.5, 52.5)" / 79 (86.5, 92, 99.5, 107.5, 116, 121.5, 128, 133.5) cm

Talamed

by Amanda Schwabe

SIZES

To Fit Actual Bust Circumference Up To: 31.5 (35.75, 39.5, 43.75, 47.5, 51.75, 55.5, 60, 64.5)" / 80 (91, 100.5, 111, 120.5, 131.5, 141, 152.5, 164) cm
2 - 8" / 5 – 20.5 cm positive ease recommended.

FINISHED MEASUREMENTS

Finished Bust Circumference: 33.5 (37.75, 41.5, 45.75, 49.5, 53.75, 57.5, 62, 66.5)" / 85 (96, 105.5, 116, 125.5, 136.5, 146, 157.5, 169) cm with front bands overlapping
Size 41.5" / 105.5 cm modelled with 7.5" / 18 cm positive ease.
Length: 28.5" / 72.5 cm from back of neck

YARN

Stolen Stitches Nua (60% Merino, 20% Linen, 20% Yak, 153 yds / 140 m per 1.76 oz / 50 g); **Colours: MC:** Angry Monkey (9807), 5 (5, 5, 6, 7, 7, 7, 8, 9) skeins; **C1:** August Storms (9809), 5 (5, 5, 6, 7, 7, 7, 8, 9) skeins; **C2:** Kitten Fluff (9810), 1 skein; **C3:** Hatter's Tea Party (9803), 1 skein; **C4:** Rolling Bales (9808), 1 skein;
Approx Yardage Used: MC: 765 (765, 765, 918, 1071, 1071, 1071, 1224, 1377) yds / 700 (700, 700, 840, 980, 980, 980, 1120, 1260) m; **C1:** 765 (765, 765, 918, 1071, 1071, 1071, 1224, 1377) yds / 700 (700, 700, 840, 980, 980, 980, 1120, 1260) m; **C2:** 153 yds / 140 m; **C3:** 153 yds / 140 m; **C4:** 153 yds / 140 m;

NEEDLES & NOTIONS

US size 5 / 3.75 mm circular needle, 32" / 80 cm long

Always use a needle size that gives you the gauge listed, as every knitter's gauge is unique.

Removable markers, tapestry needle, cable needles (2), waste yarn

GAUGE

22 sts and 40 rows = 4" / 10 cm in Garter stitch blocked

ABBREVIATIONS

See Abbreviations Section on Page 74.

TECHNIQUES & STITCH PATTERNS

See Techniques Section on Page 75 for any additional techniques not detailed in pattern.

ke

Knit elongated: knit the stitch, wrapping yarn twice around right needle to form the st instead of once. On the following row, drop the extra wrap.

pe

Purl elongated: purl the stitch, wrapping yarn twice around right needle to form the st instead of once. On the following row, drop the extra wrap.

sl

Slip purlwise. If no other direction is given, sl with yarn in back.

FC

Front cross (see Cables, below).

BC

Back cross (see Cables, below).

2-Stitch Cables

1/1 BC

Sl next st to cn and hold at back of work, k1, then k1 from cn.

1/1 FC

Sl next st to cn and hold at front of work, k1, then k1 from cn.

1/1 BCP

Sl next st to cn and hold at back of work, p1, then p1 from cn.

1/1 ke-ke FC

Sl next st to cn and hold at front of work, ke, then ke from cn.

1/1 ke-k BC

Sl next st to cn and hold at back of work, ke, then k1 from cn.

1/1 k-ke FC

Sl next st to cn and hold at front of work, k1, then ke from cn.

1/1 sl-sl BC

Sl next st to cn and hold at back of work, sl1 wyib, sl1 wyib from cn.

1/1 sl-sl FC

Sl next st to cn and hold at front of work, sl1 wyib, sl1 wyib from cn.

1/1 sl-k BC

Sl next st to cn and hold at back of work, sl1 wyib, then k1 from cn.

1/1 k-sl FC

Sl next st to cn and hold at front of work, k1, then sl1 wyib from cn.

1/1 pe-pe BC

Sl next st to cn and hold at back of work, pe, then pe from cn.

1/1 pe-pe FC

Sl next st to cn and hold at front of work, pe, then pe from cn.

1/1 k-pe BC

Sl next st to cn and hold at back of work, k1, then pe from cn.

1/1 pe-k FC

Sl next st to cn and hold at front of work, pe, then k1 from cn.

1/1 k-yfsl BC

Sl next st to cn and hold at back of work, k1, then sl1 wyif from cn.

1/1 yfsl-k FC

Sl next st to cn and hold at front of work, sl1 wyif, then k1 from cn.

1/1 ke-sl BC

Sl next st to cn and hold at back of work, ke, then sl1 wyib from cn.

1/1 sl-ke FC

Sl next st to cn and hold at front of work, sl1 wyib, then ke from cn.

1/1 ke-sl FC

Sl next st to cn and hold at front of work, ke, then sl1 wyib from cn.

1/1 sl-ke BC

Sl next st to cn and hold at back of work, sl1 wyib, then ke from cn.

3-Stitch Cables, where 1 st crosses in front of 2 sts (1/2):

1/2 sl2-sl FC

Sl next st to cn and hold at front of work, sl2 wyib, then sl1 from cn.

1/2 sl-ke2 BC

Sl next 2 sts to cn and hold at back of work, sl1 wyib, then ke twice from cn.

1/2 ke-sl2 BC

Sl next 2 sts to cn and hold at back of work, ke, then sl2 wyib from cn.

1/2 sl2-ke FC

Sl next st to cn and hold at front of work, sl2 wyib, then ke from cn.

1/2 ke2-ke FC

Sl next st to cn and hold at front of work, ke twice, then ke from cn.

3-Stitch Cables, where 2 sts cross in front of 1 st (2/1):

2/1 sl2-k BC

Sl next st to cn and hold at back of work, sl2 wyib, then k1 from cn.

2/1 k-sl2 FC

Sl next 2 sts to cn and hold at front of work, k1, then sl2 wyib from cn.

2/1 ke2-k BC

Sl next st to cn and hold at back of work, ke twice, then k1 from cn.

2/1 k-ke2 FC

Sl next 2 sts to cn and hold at front of work, k1, then ke twice from cn.

2/1 sl-sl2 FC

Sl next 2 sts to cn and hold at front of work, sl1 wyib, then sl2 wyib from cn.

2/1 ke2-ke BC

Sl next st to cn and hold at back of work, ke twice, then ke from cn.

2/1 ke-ke2 FC

Sl next 2 sts to cn and hold at front of work, ke, then ke twice from cn.

2/1 sl2-ke BC

Sl next st to cn and hold at back of work, sl2 wyib, then ke from cn.

2/1 ke-sl2 FC

Sl next 2 sts to cn and hold at front of work, ke, then sl2 wyib from cn.

2/1 ke2-sl BC

Sl next st to cn and hold at back of work, ke twice, then sl1 wyib from cn.

3-Stitch Cables, where 2 edge sts change place around centre st (1/1/1):

1/1/1 ke-k-sl BBFC

Sl next 2 sts to cn and hold at back of work, ke, sl left-most st from cn to ln, move cn with rem st to front of work, k1 from ln then sl1 wyib from cn.

1/1/1 sl-k-ke BBFC

Sl next 2 sts to cn and hold at back of work, sl1 wyib, sl left-most st from cn to ln, move cn with rem st to front of work, k1 from ln, then ke from cn.

1/1/1 ke-k-ke BBFC

Sl next 2 sts to cn and hold at back of work, ke, sl left-most st from cn to ln, move cn with rem st to front of work, k1 from ln, then ke from cn.

1/1/1 ke-k-yfsl BBC

Sl next st to cn 1 and hold at back of work, sl next st to cn 2 and hold at back, ke, k1 from cn 2, sl1 wyif from cn 1.

1/1/1 yfsl-k-ke FFC

Sl next st to cn and hold at front of work, sl next st to cn 2 and hold at front, sl1 wyif, k1 from cn 2, ke from cn 1.

Striped Garter Stitch Background

Note: *When changing colours, pick up new yarn from back.*
Row 1 (RS): Using C1, knit.
Row 2 (WS): Rep row 1.
Rows 3-4: Using MC, knit.

Slip Stitch Column (multiples of 1 st, worked over 4 rows)

All sts are slipped pwise.
C1 Row 1 (RS): Sl1 wyib.
C1 Row 2 (WS): Sl1 wyif.
MC Row 3 (RS): Ke.
MC Row 4 (WS): Sl1 wyif, dropping extra loop.
Rep Rows 1 - 4.

Notes & Tips for Travelling Sts

In the Body and Sleeves of the sweater, all the Sl Sts should be clearly visible in unbroken lines on the RS of the fabric. When they're involved in Travelling Sts, they always cross on the RS of the fabric; make sure they don't get crossed behind and lost.

Usually, a Sl St Column crosses or "travels" in front of garter sts, but sometimes, it will cross another Sl St Column; in that case, work both Columns in their own previously est'd patt after you've crossed them. The Chart indicates which column should be crossing on top.

Each line created by a Sl St Column crosses the others in an "over, under, over, under" sequence. Double check that if it went over the last time it crossed another line, it's going under the next time, and so on.

When working WS Travelling Sts in the Front Bands and Collar section, don't forget to sl wyif on RS rows, even during the crosses! Otherwise, the Column will be "strangled" on the back side.

Chart Notes

The Back Cable is divided into 5 charts due to length. Work through each chart number in order.

The Back Cable will be worked over every row down the Back, beg where indicated in Pattern Placement Set-Up Row. PM at either edge, and adjust marker placement as necessary as chart edges shift.

When working Back Cable Part 1, ensure you follow the correct Chart for your size: Sizes 1-7 use the 48-st version, size 8 uses the 52-st version and size 9 uses the 56-st version.

Back Cable Parts 2-5 are the same for all sizes.

On the Collar and Front Bands, all cables are worked on RS rows but all of the WS Sl St Column stitches are slipped wyif or worked as pe to create the reversible pattern.

PATTERN NOTES

The cardigan is worked from the top down with raglan shaping and narrow fronts; sleeves are set aside on waste yarn while the body is worked, then picked up and knit later. Wide front bands and collar are picked up and knit along the cardigan opening. The entire sweater is worked back and forth in Striped Garter Stitch; the colours change at the beginning of every RS row. The decorative cables are worked in a Slip St pattern that travels over the surface of the Garter St background, so you'll only ever use one colour for each row, while the non-matching colour gets slipped to maintain its unbroken line. To give you a chance to get used to Travelling Slipped Sts, the body cables are worked with only RS Slip Sts. The collar and fronts, however, are fully reversible and use both RS and WS Slip St Columns!

KEY FOR ALL BACK CHARTS

Key

☐ MC	▨ C1	☐ RS: knit	• WS: knit
⊺ RS: ke / WS: pe	∨ RS: sl1 wyib / WS: sl1 wyif	☐ Centre line	48 Sts
64 Sts	1/1 ke-k BC	1/1 k-ke FC	1/1 sl-k BC
1/1 FC	1/1 BC	2/1 sl-sl2 FC	1/2 sl2-sl FC
1/1 k-sl FC	1/1 ke-ke FC	1/1 sl-sl BC	1/1 sl-sl FC
1/1 ke-sl BC	1/1 sl-ke FC	1/1 sl-ke BC	1/1 ke-sl FC
1/2 ke-sl2 BC	2/1 ke2-sl BC	1/2 ke2-ke FC	2/1 ke-ke2 FC
1/2 sl2-ke FC	1/2 sl-ke2 BC	2/1 sl2-ke BC	2/1 ke-sl2 FC
2/1 sl2-k BC	2/1 k-sl2 FC	2/1 ke2-k BC	2/1 k-ke2 FC
1/1/1 sl-k-ke BBFC	1/1/1 ke-k-ke BBFC	1/1/1 ke-k-sl BBFC	∨ WS: kfb

BACK CABLE PART 1 - 48 Sts

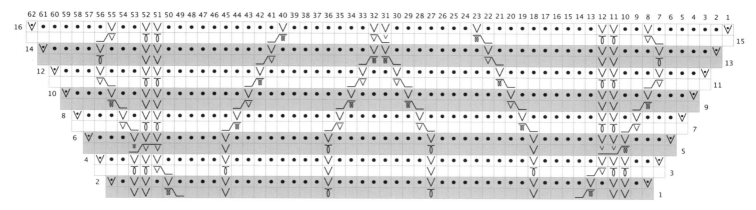

*Note: When Back Cable Part 1 - 48 Sts is **complete** you will have 64 sts between markers for Back.*

BACK CABLE PART 1 - 52 Sts

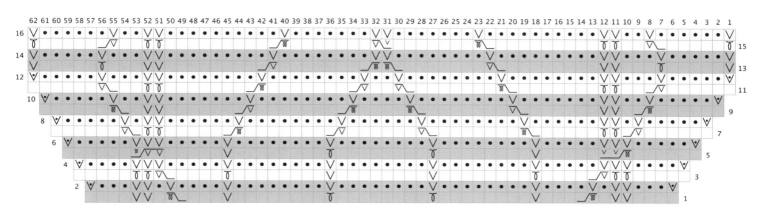

*Note: When **Row 12** of Back Cable Part 1 - 52 Sts is complete you will have 64 sts between markers for Back. You may wish to place additional markers at each side to mark position of Back Cable at this point. Subsequent increases are not shown on chart - continue to work increases as indicated in pattern, working them in Striped Garter St Background, until Back Cable Part 1 is complete.*

BACK CABLE PART 1 - 56 Sts

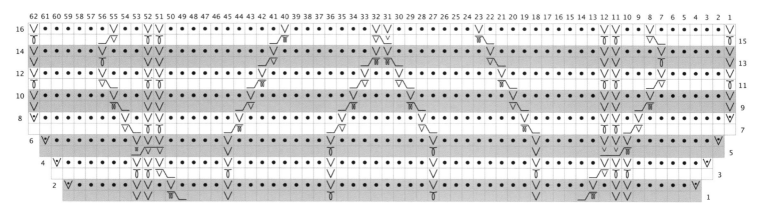

*Note: When **Row 8** of Back Cable Part 1 - 56 Sts is complete you will have 64 sts between markers for Back. You may wish to place additional markers at each side to mark position of Back Cable at this point. Subsequent increases are not shown on chart - continue to work increases as indicated in pattern, working them in Striped Garter St Background, until Back Cable Part 1 is complete.*

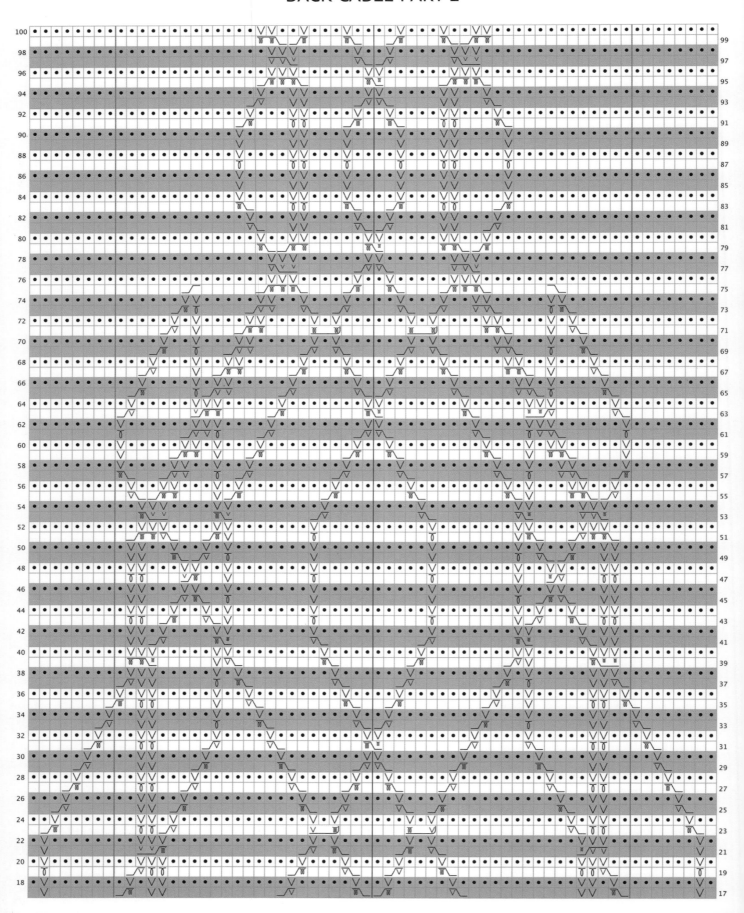

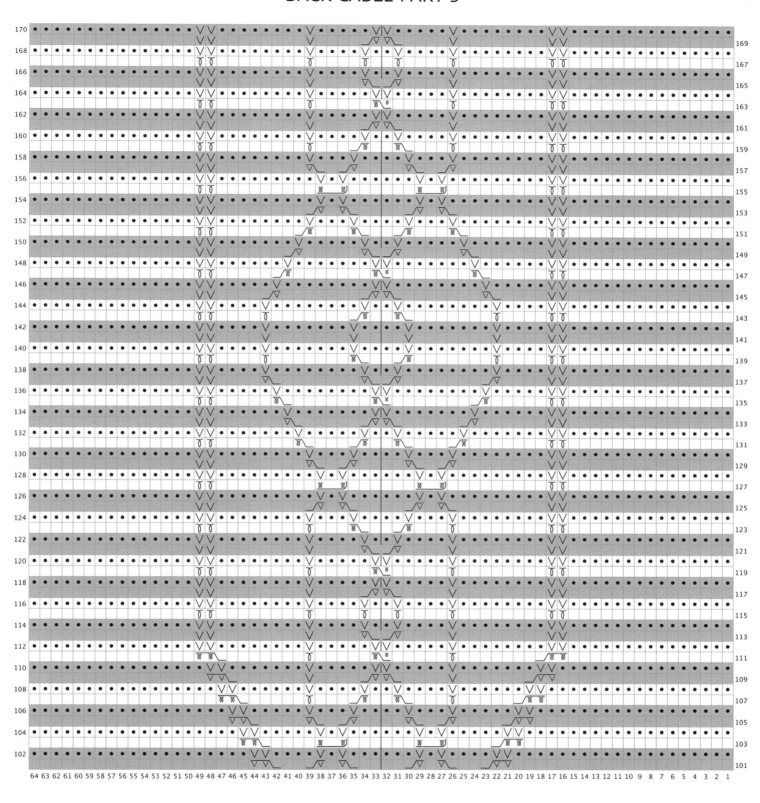

BACK CABLE PART 4

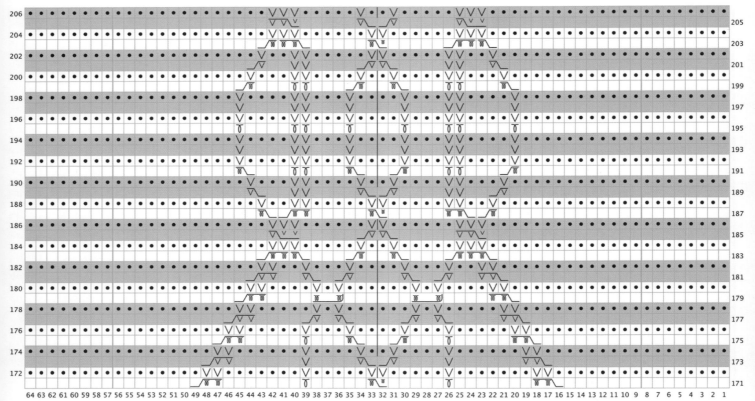

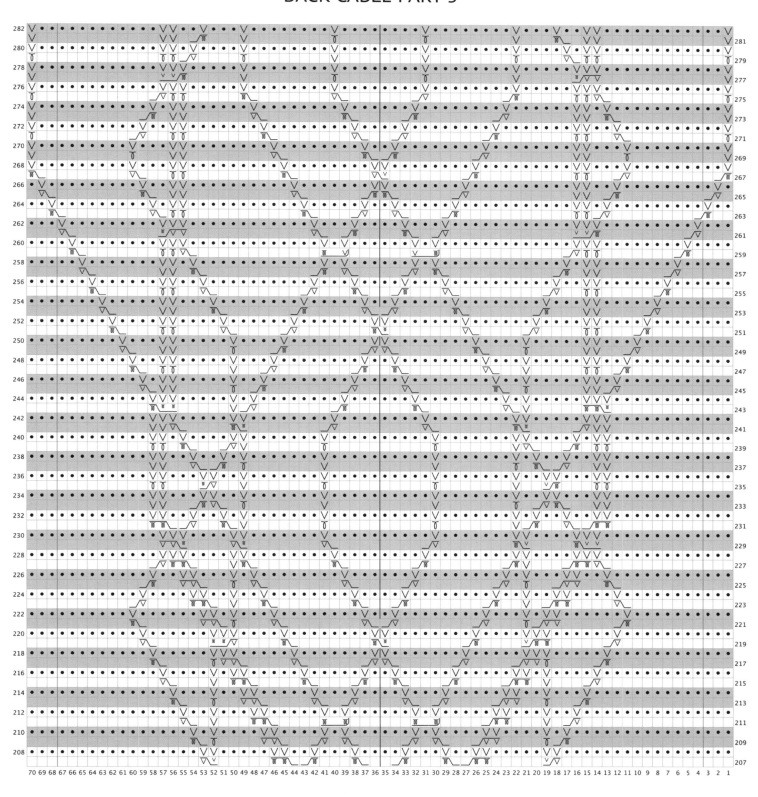

COLLAR AND FRONT BANDS CHART

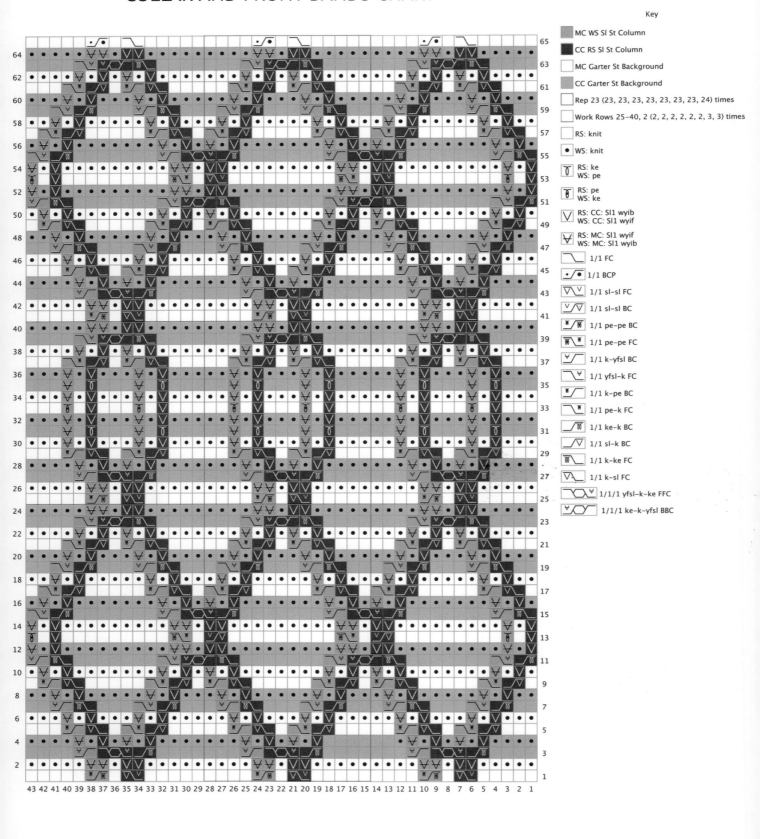

Key

- ▨ MC WS Sl St Column
- ▨ CC RS Sl St Column
- ☐ MC Garter St Background
- ▨ CC Garter St Background
- ☐ Rep 23 (23, 23, 23, 23, 23, 23, 24) times
- ☐ Work Rows 25–40, 2 (2, 2, 2, 2, 2, 3, 3) times
- ☐ RS: knit
- • WS: knit
- ▯ RS: ke / WS: pe
- ▯ RS: pe / WS: ke
- ⋁ RS: CC: Sl1 wyib / WS: CC: Sl1 wyif
- ⩔ RS: MC: Sl1 wyif / WS: MC: Sl1 wyib
- ⟍ 1/1 FC
- •⟋ 1/1 BCP
- ⋁⟍ 1/1 sl-sl FC
- ⋁⟋⋁ 1/1 sl-sl BC
- 1/1 pe-pe BC
- 1/1 pe-pe FC
- ⋁⟍ 1/1 k-yfsl BC
- ⟍ 1/1 yfsl-k FC
- 1/1 k-pe BC
- ⟍ 1/1 pe-k FC
- ⟋ 1/1 ke-k BC
- ⟋⋁ 1/1 sl-k BC
- 1/1 k-ke FC
- ⋁⟍ 1/1 k-sl FC
- ⟍⟍⋁ 1/1/1 yfsl-k-ke FFC
- ⋁⟋⟋ 1/1/1 ke-k-yfsl BBC

Row numbers (left): 64, 62, 60, 58, 56, 54, 52, 50, 48, 46, 44, 42, 40, 38, 36, 34, 32, 30, 28, 26, 24, 22, 20, 18, 16, 14, 12, 10, 8, 6, 4, 2

Row numbers (right): 65, 63, 61, 59, 57, 55, 53, 51, 49, 47, 45, 43, 41, 39, 37, 35, 33, 31, 29, 27, 25, 23, 21, 19, 17, 15, 13, 11, 9, 7, 5, 3, 1

Column numbers (bottom): 43 42 41 40 39 38 37 36 35 34 33 32 31 30 29 28 27 26 25 24 23 22 21 20 19 18 17 16 15 14 13 12 11 10 9 8 7 6 5 4 3 2 1

SLEEVE CHART

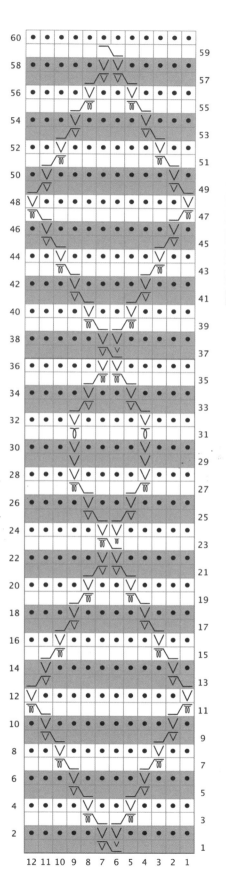

Key

☐	MC
▨	C1
☐	RS: knit
•	WS: knit
⊺	RS: ke WS: pe
V	RS: sl1 wyib WS: sl1 wyif
	1/1 sl–sl FC
	1/1 sl–k BC
	1/1 k–sl FC
	1/1 ke–k BC
	1/1 k–ke FC
	1/1 FC
	1/1 ke–ke FC
☐	work rows 1– 36 twice

PATTERN

Note: You may want to review the Slip Stitch Column Technique on page 55.

RAGLAN YOKE SHAPING

Using MC, CO 72 (72, 72, 72, 72, 72, 72, 76, 80) sts.

Marker Set-Up Row (RS): K2, pm, k1, pm, k8, pm, k1, pm, k48 (48, 48, 48, 48, 48, 48, 52, 56), pm, k1, pm, k8, pm, k1, pm, k2. This sets marker placement and sts are arranged as: front, m, Slip Stitch Column seam, m, sleeve, m, Slip Stitch Column seam, m, back, m, Slip Stitch Column seam, m, sleeve, m, Slip Stitch Column seam, m, front. Slip markers on all following rows.

Next Row (WS): Knit.

Join C1 and begin working in Striped Garter Stitch Background and set up pattern elements as follows:

Pattern Placement Set-Up Row (RS): Knit to m, sl m, work Sl St Column, sl m, knit to m, sl m, work Sl St Column, sl m, work back sts working Back Chart over centre 48 (48, 48, 48, 48, 48, 48, 52, 56) sts, sl m, work Sl St Column, sl m, knit to m, sl m, work Sl St Column, sl m, knit to end.

You may find that the Sl St Column "seams" are marker enough on their own; they will always be worked in MC and so will stand out from the Striped Garter St background.

On WS Rows, every background st is knit, and all sl sts are slipped purlwise with the yarn in front. The sl sts are recognizable with a little experience: they are either the opposite colour of the yarn you're using, or they're an elongated st and need to have the extra loop dropped as they're slipped. Until you can recognize them, feel free to mark them in some way.

You'll now cont in patt, maintaining Sl St Columns and Back Chart as est'd and begin raglan shaping.

Read the entire following yoke section carefully before beginning as you'll be working multiple sets of raglan shaping and establishing the Sleeve Chart at the same time.

Raglan shaping happens on WS rows, using kfb to increase 1 st at both edges of each Sleeve, both edges of the Back, and 1 st at the sleeve-adjacent edge of each Front. The kfb increases should be directly beside the Sl St Column "seams".

Back Chart Part 1 expands as you increase, and includes some of the intial kfb increases; during Part 2, increases are not shown and should be worked in Striped Garter Stitch Background as est'd. As you increase in the back section, you may wish to place additional markers on each side of the Back Chart to mark its beginning and end.

The following two rows indicate how to increase for the Sleeves and Body. Read through them carefully without knitting, then work them the correct number of times for your size, noting that Sleeve and Body increases will often be worked on the same row.

Sleeve Increase Row (WS): Patt to m, sl m, work Sl St Column, sl m, kfb, patt to last st before m, kfb, sl m, work Sl St Column, sl m, patt to m, sl m, work Sl St Column, sl m, kfb, patt to last st before m, kfb, sl m, work Sl St Column, sl m, patt to end. *4 Sleeve sts inc'd.*

Body Increase Row (WS): Patt to last st before m, kfb, sl m, work Sl St Column, sl m, patt to m, sl m, work Sl St Column, sl m, kfb, patt to last st before m, kfb, sl m, work Sl St Column, sl m, patt to m, sl m, work Sl St Column, sl m, kfb, patt to end. *4 Body sts inc'd.*

Work Sleeve Increase Row on every WS row 10 (5, 6, 16, 21, 24, 25, 31, 31) times, then every other WS row 11 (15, 16, 12, 11, 10, 11, 8, 9) times. *50 (48, 52, 64, 72, 76, 80, 86, 88) sts per Sleeve.*

At the same time, work Body Increase Row every WS row 8 (8, 10, 20, 25, 34, 41, 47, 49) times, then every other WS row 7 (12, 14, 10, 9, 5, 3, 0, 0) times. *78 (88, 96, 108, 116, 126, 136, 146, 154) sts in Back, 17 (22, 26, 32, 36, 41, 46, 49, 51) sts in Front.*

Sleeve Chart

At the same time as the Raglan Shaping, when piece measures 4.5" / 11.5 cm from cast-on and after working a WS row in MC, begin working Sleeve Chart over centre 12 sts on each Sleeve. Continue working through Sleeve Chart as established throughout.

Once all shaping has been completed, there are 33 (36, 39, 41, 44, 45, 48, 48, 50) Garter ridges worked, ending after a WS row, and a total of 216 (232, 256, 304, 336, 364, 392, 420, 436) sts.

Divide Sleeves from Body

Make a note on Sleeve Chart of which rows you've completed, so you can resume at the correct place later.

Dividing Row (RS): K17 (22, 26, 32, 36, 41, 46, 49, 51), sl m, work Sl St Column, sl m, place next 50 (48, 52, 64, 72, 76, 80, 86, 88) sts on waste yarn, CO 10 (12, 14, 14, 16, 18, 18, 20, 22) sts using Backwards Loop Method, sl m, work Sl St Column, sl m, work 78 (88, 96, 108, 116, 126, 136, 146, 154) Back sts in patt, sl m, work Sl St Column, sl m, place next 50 (48, 52, 64, 72, 76, 80, 86, 88) sts on waste yarn, CO 10 (12, 14, 14, 16, 18, 18, 20, 22) sts using Backwards Loop Method, sl m, work Sl St Column, sl m, k17 (22, 26, 32, 36, 41, 46, 49, 51). *136 (160, 180, 204, 224, 248, 268, 288, 304) sts.*

Next Row (WS): Cont in patt as est'd, working in Striped Garter St Background, maintaining the 4 Sl St Columns, the Back Chart in the centre of the Back sts, and working the CO sts in Striped Garter St Background (These sts will now be called Side Panels).

BODY

Work even in est'd patt until Body measures 7 (7.25, 7.5, 7.5, 7.5, 7.5, 7.5, 7.5, 7.5)" / 18 (18.5, 19, 19, 19, 19, 19, 19, 19) cm from underarm CO or until the sweater hits your narrowest waist measurement when tried on, ending with a RS row.

A-Line Shaping (Optional)

Work the following shaping if your Hip measurement is larger than your Bust measurement:
Increases are placed at the edges of the Side Panels, directly adjacent to the Sl St Columns, on a WS row.
Hip Inc Row (WS): *Patt to m, sl m, Sl St Column, sl m, kfb, patt to last st before m, kfb, sl m, Sl St Column, sl m; rep from * once, patt to end. *4 sts inc'd.*
Work Hip Inc Row every 20th row twice more. *148 (172, 192, 216, 236, 260, 280, 300, 316) sts; 16 (18, 20, 20, 22, 24, 24, 26, 28) sts in each Side Panel.*

Work even in patt as est'd until Back Chart is complete.
Next Row (RS): Using MC, knit to end.
Bind off on the WS using MC.

SLEEVES

For ease of knitting, Sleeves are worked flat in Striped Garter St Background and then seamed. The contrasting cuff measures 5" / 12.5 cm in length.

Transfer Sleeve sts from waste yarn to needles. Using the correct colour to maintain Striped Garter St Background on the top of the Sleeve cap, and beginning at centre of armhole cast-on sts with RS facing, pick up and knit 5 (6, 7, 7, 8, 9, 9, 10, 11) sts from cast-on sts, work across Sleeve sts in patt (resuming Sleeve Chart where you left off), pick up and knit 5 (6, 7, 7, 8, 9, 9, 10, 11) sts from cast-on sts. *60 (60, 66, 78, 88, 94, 98, 106, 110) sts.*

Work even in patt until Sleeve measures 4" / 10 cm from armhole CO sts.

Sleeve Shaping

Sleeve Dec Row (RS): K2, k2tog, work in patt to last 4 sts, ssk, k2. *2 sts dec'd.*
Rep Dec Row every 8 (10, 8, 6, 6, 4, 4, 4, 4)th row 12 (10, 13, 17, 20, 22, 23, 26, 28) more times. *34 (38, 38, 42, 46, 48, 50, 52, 52) sts.*

At the same time, when Sleeve measures 11.5 (12, 12, 12.5, 12.5, 13, 13, 13.5, 13.5)" / 29 (30.5, 30.5, 32, 32, 33, 33, 34.5, 34.5) cm from armhole cast-on sts and after a C1 WS row, join C4 and cut MC and knit 2 rows in C4, then 2 rows in C1, then cut C1 and cont to end using C4 only.

Cont even Garter St (no striping) until Sleeve measures approx 16.5 (17, 17, 17.5, 17.5, 18, 18, 18.5, 18.5)" / 42 (43, 43, 44.5, 44.5, 45.5, 45.5, 47, 47) cm from underarm cast-on sts or until desired length, ending after a RS row. Bind off on the WS.

Rep for second Sleeve.

FRONT BANDS AND COLLAR

In this section, you'll still be working the Striped Garter St Background and Travelling Sts, but now the pattern will include WS Slip Stitch Columns (see Techniques & Stitch Patterns) to make the Fronts and Collar reversible.
Read through all directions before beginning as colour changes happen at the same time as chart being worked.

Using C1 and with RS facing, starting at bottom edge of Right Front, pick up and knit 143 sts (approx. 1 st in each garter ridge bump) along Right Front, pick up and knit 72 (72, 72, 72, 72, 72, 72, 76, 80) sts from neck edge cast-on, pick and up knit 143 sts along Left Front.
358 (358, 358, 358, 358, 358, 358, 362, 366) sts.

Row 1 (WS): K1, kfb, k143, kfb, knit to last 2 sts, kfb, k1.
361 (361, 361, 361, 361, 361, 361, 365, 369) sts.
Row 2 (RS): Join MC and working in Striped Garter St Background, k5 (5, 5, 5, 5, 5, 5, 7, 2), pm, work Collar and Fronts Chart to last 5 (5, 5, 5, 5, 5, 5, 7, 2) sts, pm, knit to end. The markers placed in this row are meant to indicate the Chart beginning and end.
Row 3 (WS): K1, kfb, knit to m, sl m, work Chart as est'd, sl m, knit to last 2 sts, kfb, k1. *2 sts inc'd.*
Row 4 (RS): Knit to m, sl m, work Chart, sl m, knit to end.

Rep rows 3 & 4, ending after a Row 3, until all Chart rows for your size have been worked as follows:
Work Chart Rows 1-24 once, then work Chart Rows 25-40 a total of 2 (2, 2, 2, 2, 2, 2, 3, 3) times through, then work Chart Rows 41-65 once. (For a deeper or narrower Front Band and Collar, work more or less repeats of rows 25-40. Each 16-row rep adds about 1.5" / 4 cm of depth.)

At the same time, while working the last rep through Chart Rows 25-40 for your size, replace C1 with C2 starting on a row 27 (27, 27, 27, 27, 27, 27, 35, 35), and then replace MC with C3 starting on a row 33 (33, 33, 33, 33, 33, 33, 41, 41). Break C1 and MC and cont in patt using C2 and C3 to end.

BO kwise on WS using C3.

FINISHING

Sew Sleeve seams using mattress stitch. Weave in ends.
Wash and block to measurements. Wear open or fastened
overlapping with a shawl pin.

SCHEMATIC

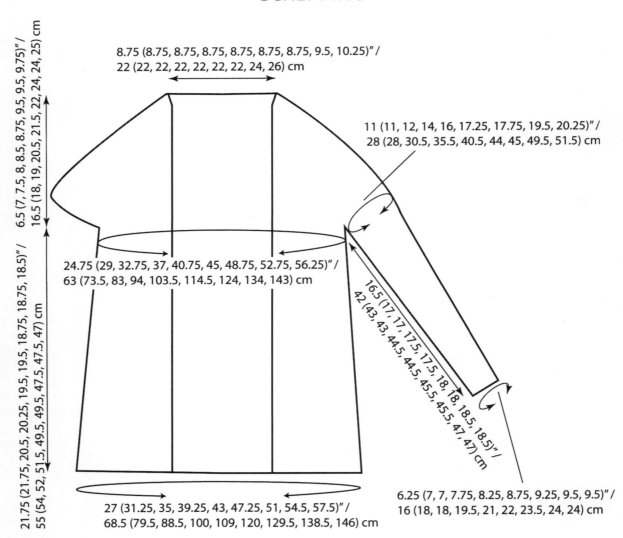

8.75 (8.75, 8.75, 8.75, 8.75, 8.75, 8.75, 9.5, 10.25)" /
22 (22, 22, 22, 22, 22, 22, 24, 26) cm

11 (11, 12, 14, 16, 17.25, 17.75, 19.5, 20.25)" /
28 (28, 30.5, 35.5, 40.5, 44, 45, 49.5, 51.5) cm

6.5 (7, 7.5, 8, 8.5, 8.75, 9.5, 9.5, 9.75)" /
16.5 (18, 19, 20.5, 21.5, 22, 24, 24, 25) cm

24.75 (29, 32.75, 37, 40.75, 45, 48.75, 52.75, 56.25)" /
63 (73.5, 83, 94, 103.5, 114.5, 124, 134, 143) cm

21.75 (21.75, 20.5, 20.25, 19.5, 19.5, 18.75, 18.75, 18.5)" /
55 (54, 52, 51.5, 49.5, 49.5, 47.5, 47.5, 47) cm

16.5 (17, 17, 17.5, 17.5, 18, 18, 18.5, 18.5)" /
42 (43, 43, 44.5, 44.5, 45.5, 45.5, 47, 47) cm

6.25 (7, 7, 7.75, 8.25, 8.75, 9.25, 9.5, 9.5)" /
16 (18, 18, 19.5, 21, 22, 23.5, 24, 24) cm

27 (31.25, 35, 39.25, 43, 47.25, 51, 54.5, 57.5)" /
68.5 (79.5, 88.5, 100, 109, 120, 129.5, 138.5, 146) cm

Note: Front Collar not shown.

Áine
by Isabell Kraemer

SIZES

1 (2, 3, 4, 5, 6, 7, 8)
To Fit Bust Circumference Up To: 32.75 (36.25, 39.5, 41.75, 44.75, 48, 50, 52.25)" / 83 (92, 100.5, 106, 113.5, 122, 127, 132.5) cm
3 - 7" / 7.5 - 18 cm positive ease recommended.

FINISHED MEASUREMENTS

Finished Bust Circumference: 35.75 (39.25, 42.5, 44.75, 47.75, 51, 53, 55.25)" / 91 (99.5, 108, 113.5, 121.5, 129.5, 134.5, 140.5) cm
Size 42.5" / 108 cm modeled with 7.5" / 19 cm of positive ease.

YARN

Stolen Stitches 'Nua' (60% Merino, 20% Linen, 20% Yak, 153 yds / 140 m per 1.76 oz / 50g); **Colours: MC:** August Storms (9809), 7 (8, 9, 9, 10, 11, 11, 12) skeins; **CC:** Rolling Bales (9808), 1 skein;
Approx Yardage Used: MC: 1012 (1126, 1228, 1308, 1422, 1536, 1638, 1729) yds / 932 (1038, 1132, 1205, 1310, 1415, 1509, 1592) m; **CC:** 57 (62, 64, 71, 73, 80, 82, 84) yds / 52 (57, 59, 65, 67, 74, 76, 78) m

NEEDLES & NOTIONS

US 5 / 3.75 mm circular needle, 16" / 40 cm and 32" / 80 cm long
US 5 / 3.75 mm DPNs
US 4 / 3.5 mm circular needle, 16" / 40 cm and 32" / 80 cm long
US 4 / 3.5 mm DPNs

Always use a needle size that gives you the gauge listed, as every knitter's gauge is unique.

Stitch holders, stitch markers, tapestry needles, blocking tools

GAUGE

22 sts and 33 rows = 4" / 10 cm in St St & St St Colour Work blocked using larger needle

ABBREVIATIONS

See Abbreviations Section on Page 74.

TECHNIQUES & STITCH PATTERNS

See Techniques Section on Page 75 for any additional techniques not detailed in pattern.

Colour Work Chart

Multiple of 10 sts
Chart is to be read from bottom to top and from right to left.

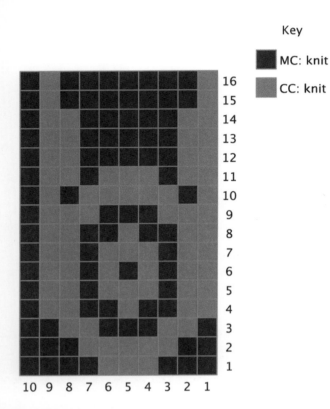

Key

■ MC: knit

■ CC: knit

PATTERN NOTES

This jumper is worked seamlessly from the top down. First some short rows are worked back and forth to create a higher back neck and then the round yoke is worked top down with a striking colour work band to sleeve separation. Some last short rows are worked to finish the yoke shaping right before sleeve stitches are placed on hold in order to work the body first down to the hem. Sleeves are worked top down in rounds to the cuffs last.

PATTERN

YOKE

With MC and short US 4 / 3.5 mm needle, CO 106 (110, 114, 114, 114, 118, 118, 120) sts, using your preferred method. Join to work in the rnd (being careful not to twist stitches) and place marker for BOR (rnds beg at centre of back).
Next Rnd: *K1, p1; rep from * to end.
Rep last rnd 5 more times.

Change to short US 5 / 3.75 mm needle.
Size 1: K10, *k8, M1L; rep from * to end. *12 sts inc'd.*
Size 2: K11, M1L, *k9, M1L; rep from * to end. *12 sts inc'd.*
Sizes 3 & 4: *K9, M1L, k10, M1L; rep from * to end. *12 sts inc'd.*
Size 5: K6, M1L, *k9, M1L; rep from * to end. *13 sts inc'd.*
Sizes 6 & 7: K8, M1L, *k10, M1L; rep from * to end. *12 sts inc'd.*
Size 8: K12, M1L, *k9, M1L; rep from * to end. *13 sts inc'd.*
118 (122, 126, 126, 127, 130, 130, 133) sts.

All Sizes: Knit one rnd.

Note: Change to a longer circular needle when needed to accommodate the increasing number of stitches.

Short Row Shaping

Short Row 1 (RS): K30 (32, 33, 33, 34, 36, 38, 38), turn work.
Short Row 2 (WS): Work German Short Row, purl to m, sl m, p30 (32, 33, 33, 34, 36, 38, 38), turn work.
Short Row 3 (RS): Work German Short Row, knit to m, sl m, * k4, M1L; rep from * 0 (3, 3, 2, 3, 4, 6, 7) more time(s), knit to double stitch, knit double stitch, k3, turn work.
Short Row 4 (WS): Work German Short Row, purl to m, sl m, *p4, M1Lp; rep from * 0 (3, 3, 2, 3, 4, 6, 7) more time(s), purl to double stitch, purl double stitch, p3, turn work.
Short Row 5 (RS): Work German Short Row, knit to m, sl m, knit to double stitch, knit double stitch, k2, turn work.
Short Row 6 (WS): Work German Short Row, purl to m, sl m, purl to double stitch, purl double stitch, p2, turn work.
Rep Short Rows 5 & 6 two more times.
Next row (RS): Work German Short Row, knit to m, sl m.
120 (130, 134, 132, 135, 140, 144, 149) sts.
Continue working in rnds (work double stitch as single stitch when you pass). Knit 2 rnds.

Inc Set 1

Sizes 1, 2 & 3: Continue to Inc Set 2.
Size 4: *K5, M1L, k6; rep from * to end. *12 sts inc'd.*
Knit 6 rnds.
Size 5: *K4, M1L, k5; rep from * to end. *15 sts inc'd.*
Knit 6 rnds.
Size 6: *K3, M1L, k4; rep from * to end. *20 sts inc'd.*
Knit 8 rnds.
Size 7: *[K7, M1L] 4 times, k8, M1L; rep from * to end. *20 sts inc'd.*
Knit 8 rnds.
Size 8: K1, *k3, M1L, k4; rep from * to 1 stitch before end, k1. *21 sts inc'd.*
Knit 10 rnds.
- (-, -, 144, 150, 160, 164, 170) sts.

Inc Set 2

All Sizes: *K2, M1L; rep from * to end. *60 (65, 67, 72, 75, 80, 82, 85) sts inc'd; 180 (195, 201, 216, 225, 240, 246, 255) sts.*
Knit 6 (6, 6, 8, 8, 8, 8, 8) rnds.

Inc Set 3

Sizes 1, 2, 5, 6 & 8: *K3, M1L; rep from * to end. *60 (65, -, -, 75, 80, -, 85) sts inc'd.*
Sizes 3, 4 & 7: [K2, M1L] 3 times, *k3, M1L; rep from * to 6 sts before end, [k2, M1L] 3 times. *- (-, 69, 74, -, -, 84, -) sts inc'd 240 (260, 270, 290, 300, 320, 330, 340) sts.*
Knit 4 rnds.

Colour Work Band

Attach CC and work Rnd 1 to 16 from chart. Break CC and continue in MC to end.

Inc Set 4

All Sizes: K5, M1L, *k10, M1L; rep from * to 5 sts before end, k5. *24 (26, 27, 29, 30, 32, 33, 34) sts inc'd; 264 (286, 297, 319, 330, 352, 363, 374) sts.*
Knit 4 (6, 6, 8, 8, 8, 8, 8) rnds.

Inc Set 5

Size 1: *K66, M1L; rep from * to end. *4 sts inc'd.*
Size 2: K17, M1L, *k28, M1L; rep from * to 17 sts before end, k17. *10 sts inc'd.*
Size 3: K8, M1L, *k14, M1L; rep from * to 9 sts before end, k9. *21 sts inc'd.*
Size 4: K16, M1L, *k13, M1L; rep from * to 17 sts before end, k17. *23 sts inc'd.*
Size 5: *K10, M1L; rep from * to 10 sts before end, k10. *32 sts inc'd.*
Size 6: *K11, M1L; rep from * to end. *32 sts inc'd.*
Size 7: *K11, M1L; rep from * to end. *33 sts inc'd.*
Size 8: *K11, M1L; rep from * to end. *34 sts inc'd.*
268 (296, 318, 342, 362, 384, 396, 408) sts.

All Sizes: Work in St St in rnds until yoke measures 7.25 (7.75, 8, 8.25, 8.75, 9.25, 9.75, 10)" / 18.5 (19.5, 20.5, 21, 22, 23.5, 24.5, 25.5) cm measured at the centre back.

Finish Yoke Shaping

Short Row 1 (RS): K41 (46, 50, 53, 56, 60, 62, 64), pm, k51 (55, 58, 64, 68, 71, 73, 75), pm, k5 (5, 5, 5, 5, 6, 6, 7), turn work.
Short Row 2 (WS): Work German Short Row, *purl to m, sl m; rep from * 2 more times, p42 (47, 51, 54, 57, 61, 63, 65), pm, p51 (55, 58, 64, 68, 71, 73, 75), pm, p5 (5, 5, 5, 5, 6, 6, 7), turn work.
Short Row 3 (RS): Work German Short Row, *knit to m, sl m; rep from * 4 more times, knit to double stitch, knit double stitch, k4, turn work.
Short Row 4 (WS): Work German Short Row, *purl to m, sl m; rep from * 4 more times, purl to double stitch, purl double stitch, p4, turn work.
Rep Short Rows 3 & 4 two more times.
Next Row (RS): Work German Short Row, knit to BOR m. Resume working in the round (work double stitch as single stitch when you pass).
Knit 1 rnd.

Separate Sleeves and Body

Division Rnd: Remove BOR marker, knit to next m, remove m, place 51 (55, 58, 64, 68, 71, 73, 75) Sleeve sts on a holder or waste yarn, using the Backwards Loop Cast-On, CO 8 (8, 8, 8, 9, 10, 11, 12) sts, pm (new BOR marker), CO 7 (7, 8, 8, 9, 9, 10, 11) sts, remove m, knit across Front sts, remove m, place 51 (55, 58, 64, 68, 71, 73, 75) Sleeve sts on a holder or waste yarn, using the Backwards Loop Cast-On, CO 15 (15, 16, 16, 18, 19, 21, 23) sts, remove m, knit across Back to new BOR m.
196 (216, 234, 246, 262, 280, 292, 304) sts.

BODY

Continue working in St St in the rnd until Body measures 13 (13, 13, 13, 13.5, 13.5, 14, 14)" / 33 (33, 33, 33, 34, 34, 35.5, 35.5) cm, or 2.75" / 7 cm less than desired length from underarm CO.

Hem

Change to long US 4 / 3.5 mm needle.
Rnd 1: * K1, p1; rep from * to end.
Rep Rnd 1 until hem measures 2.75" / 7 cm.
Knit 1 rnd. BO knitwise.

SLEEVES

Divide held Sleeve stitches evenly over 3 US 5 / 3.75 mm DPNs. With fourth DPN, pick up and knit 15 (15, 16, 16, 18, 19, 21, 23) sts from underarm cast on. Join for working in the rnd and place a marker in the centre of the picked up underarm stitches. *66 (70, 74, 80, 86, 90, 94, 98) Sleeve sts.*

Note: You may want to pick up additional stitches at each side of the underarm CO stitches to avoid holes at these points. Please decrease these additional stitches in first rnd to achieve the right stitch count for your sleeves.

Work in St St in the rnd until Sleeve measures 3" / 7.5 cm from underarm.

Dec Rnd: K2, k2tog, knit to 4 sts before m, ssk, k2. *2 sts dec'd.*
Rep Dec rnd every 13th (11th, 10th, 8th, 7th, 6th, 6th, 5th) rnd 7 (8, 9, 12, 14, 16, 17, 19) more times.
50 (52, 54, 54, 56, 56, 58, 58) Sleeve sts.
Continue in St St in the rnd until Sleeve measures 16.5" / 42 cm, or 1.5" / 4 cm less than desired length from underarm.

Cuff

Change to US 4 / 3.5 mm DPNs.
Rnd 1: * K1, p1; rep from * to end.
Rep Rnd 1 until Cuff measures 1.5" / 4 cm.
Knit one rnd. BO knitwise.

Rep instructions for second sleeve.

FINISHING

Block sweater to measurements and weave in ends.

SCHEMATIC

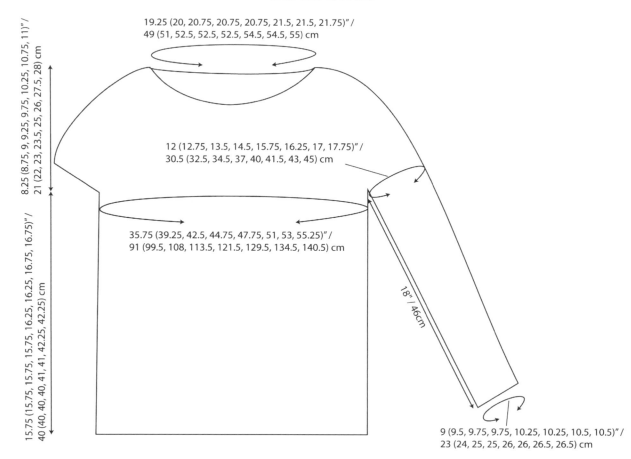

19.25 (20, 20.75, 20.75, 20.75, 21.5, 21.5, 21.75)" / 49 (51, 52.5, 52.5, 52.5, 54.5, 54.5, 55) cm

8.25 (8.75, 9, 9.25, 9.75, 10.25, 10.75, 11)" / 21 (22, 23, 23.5, 25, 26, 27.5, 28) cm

12 (12.75, 13.5, 14.5, 15.75, 16.25, 17, 17.75)" / 30.5 (32.5, 34.5, 37, 40, 41.5, 43, 45) cm

35.75 (39.25, 42.5, 44.75, 47.75, 51, 53, 55.25)" / 91 (99.5, 108, 113.5, 121.5, 129.5, 134.5, 140.5) cm

18" / 46cm

15.75 (15.75, 15.75, 15.75, 16.25, 16.25, 16.75, 16.75)" / 40 (40, 40, 40, 41, 41, 42.25, 42.25) cm

9 (9.5, 9.75, 9.75, 10.25, 10.25, 10.5, 10.5)" / 23 (24, 25, 25, 26, 26, 26.5, 26.5) cm

Abbreviations

*_;	repeat directions from * as indicated		**patt**	pattern
[]	repeat directions within brackets as indicated		**pm**	place marker
"	Inches		**p**	purl
approx	approximately		**pwise**	purl wise
Beg	begin(ning)		**pe**	elongated purl stitch
BOR	beginning of the rnd		**p2tog**	purl 2 stitches together
BO	bind off (cast off)		**p3tog**	purl 3 stitches together
CC	contrast colour		**pfb**	purl into front and back of stitch
cn	cable needle		**rem**	remaining
CO	cast on		**rep**	repeat
cm	centimetre		**rev**	reverse
circ	circular needle		**Rev St St**	reverse stocking (stockinette) stitch
dm	dart marker		**RH**	right hand
dec('d)	decrease(d)		**rn**	right needle
dpn(s)	double pointed needle(s)		**RLI(p)**	Right Lifted Increase, knit (or purl)
est'd	established		**RS**	right side(s)
g	grams		**rnd(s)**	round(s)
inc('d)	increase(d)		**SR**	short row
k	knit		**sl**	slip
ke	elongated knit stitch		**ssk**	slip 2 sts, one at a time, as if to knit, then knit those 2 stitches together through the back loops
k2tog	knit 2 stitches together		**ssp**	slip 2 sts, one at a time, as if to knit, then purl those 2 stitches together through the back loops
ktog	knit together			
kfb	knit into front and back of stitch		**sssk**	slip 3 stitches, one at a time, as if to knit, then knit those 3 stitches together through the back loops
kwise	knit wise			
LH	left hand		**st(s)**	stitch(es)
ln	left needle		**St St**	stocking (stockinette) stitch
LLI(p)	Left Lifted Increase, knit (or purl)		**tbl**	through back loops
MC	main colour		**wyib**	with yarn in back
M1	make one		**wyif**	with yarn in front
M1L(p)	Make 1 Left, knit or purl		**WS**	wrong side(s)
M1R(p)	Make 1 Right, knit or purl		**yd(s)**	yard(s)
meas	measures		**yo**	yarn over
m	marker / metre(s) only used in yardage		**1-into-3**	make 3 sts from 1
mm	millimetres		**1-into-5**	make 5 sts from 1
p2sso	pass 2 slipped sts over			

Techniques

CAST-ONS

When no cast-on is specified you should use your preferred cast-on method. The Long Tail Cast-On is useful for most situations.

Backwards Loop Cast-On

Begin by placing a slip knot on the needle. *With the working yarn twist a loop backwards in the yarn, place the loop on the needle and pull the working yarn to tighten the stitch up; repeat from * until the desired number of stitches have been cast on.

Long Tail Cast-On

Begin by leaving a long tail. Typically three times the length of the cast-on you are working. This cast-on uses only one needle held in front of you.
1. Create a slip knot and tighten it onto your needle. Keep your working yarn to your right and your yarn tail to your left. Hold needle in right hand.
2. With your left hand using the yarn tail, bring your thumb from behind the yarn, scoop it up and slide the loop created onto the needle. Leave your thumb in position.
3. With your right hand with the working yarn, bring the yarn around under the needle and wrap it on top (as though to knit a stitch). Keep holding this yarn in position.
4. With your left thumb (still in the first loop), lift this thumb over the end of the needle, scooping the initial loop you created over the second loop. Tighten both ends of the yarn until you are happy with the tension of the stitch.

Repeat steps 2-4 until you have the correct number of stitches on the needle.

https://stolenstitches.com/blogs/tutorials/long-tail-cast-on

Knitted Cast-On

If you are starting with no stitches on the needle create a slip knot, knit into the slip knot, place the stitch created from right to left needle. *Knit into the first stitch, slip the new stitch created from right to left needle; repeat from * until the desired number of stitches have been cast on. If you are casting on with stitches already on the needle you can began at *.

Provisional Cast-Ons
Crochet Method

This cast-on method uses waste yarn and a crochet hook to create a crochet chain that wraps a stitch around your knitting needle at the same time. It is not necessary to know how to crochet to use this method.

Make a slip knot with waste yarn and place on crochet hook. Hold crochet hook above the needle; *wrap yarn under and around the needle and then wrap yarn over crochet hook and pull through the stitch on the hook*. There is one stitch on the needle and one stitch on the hook.

Repeat from * to * until you have the appropriate number of stitches on the needle.

When you have cast on the correct number of stitches, cut yarn, pull end of yarn through final stitch on crochet hook and put a knot at end of yarn to mark the end where you will begin unravelling the chain.

Switch to the project yarn and begin knitting.

When you need to remove the Provisional Cast-On, unravel the crochet chain starting at the knotted end. Carefully place each of the live stitches exposed on a needle and begin working as instructed.

http://www.stolenstitches.com/tutorials/cast-ons/provisional-cast-on-crochet-method/

Invisible Cast-On Method

This method can use either waste yarn or a second circular needle to hold the second set of stitches. You do need to be careful with this cast-on when working from the held stitches that every other stitch is mounted backwards.

Tie the working yarn and waste yarn together. With your left hand hold waste yarn with index finger and keep working yarn below thumb.

The cast-on is a 2 step process:

Step 1: Put needle between yarns and scoop working yarn from below and around front to put first stitch on needle.
Step 2: Lift needle over and behind waste yarn and bring around to the front of the working yarn and scoop the working yarn from underneath to put the second stitch on the needle.

Repeat these 2 stitches until you have the desired number of stitches.

https://stolenstitches.com/blogs/tutorials/provisional-cast-on-invisible-method

SHORT ROWS

There are several different ways of working short rows. The method used in each pattern is usually specified. You can find details below on two different types of short rows.

Wrap And Turn (w&t)

On a knit row:
Knit to the turning point and slip the next stitch from left to right needle purlwise.
Pass yarn from back to front of work and slip stitch back from right to left needle.
Turn your work to purl side, passing yarn from back to front of work. When you work the next stitch, take care to pull yarn snugly.

On a purl row:
Purl to turning point and slip next stitch from left to right needle purlwise.
Pass yarn from front to back of work and slip stitch back from right to left needle.
Turn your work to knit side, passing yarn from front to back of work.

When you come to a wrapped stitch in subsequent rows:

For knit stitches: Lift the wrap with the right needle from the front, lifting from bottom to top of the wrap.
With wrap still on right needle, insert right needle into front of wrapped stitch and knit the wrap together with the stitch.
For purl stitches: Lift the wrap with right needle from the right-side of the work, lifting from bottom to top of the wrap, and sit it on the left needle. Purl the wrap together with the stitch that was wrapped.

https://stolenstitches.com/blogs/tutorials/wrap-turn

German Short Rows

Work to turning point, turn work. Slip 1 stitch purlwise from left to right needle with yarn in front. Pull yarn over needle to back of work, creating a 'double stitch' on the right needle. Bring yarn to correct side of work for knit/purl, ensuring the double-stitch stays in place.

When you encounter this 'double stitch' on a following row, work it as a single stitch, working it into the pattern as needed.

http://www.stolenstitches.com/tutorials/short-rows/german-short-rows-in-garter-stitch/

CABLES

Throughout this book cables are used frequently,. The specific directions to work each cable are given within the pattern. You can either use a cable needle (cn) or work without a cable needle if you prefer.

You can find general information on working cables here:

https://stolenstitches.com/blogs/tutorials/tagged/cables

GRAFTING

When you wish to join 2 pieces of knitting together seamlessly you can use grafting (Kitchener Stitch). This graft mimics a row of knitting. This means that the type of stitches you are joining together will determine how you work a graft.

Grafting in Stocking Stitch

Place an equal number of stitches on the front and back needles; break yarn leaving a generous tail, approximately 3 times the length of your work. Thread a tapestry needle with the yarn to the right of the stitches.

Step 1: Pull needle through first front stitch as if to purl, leave stitch on needle.
Step 2: Pull needle through first back stitch as if to knit, leave stitch on needle.
Step 3: Pull needle through first front stitch as if to knit and slip stitch off needle. Pull needle through next front stitch as if to purl, leave stitch on needle.
Step 4: Pull needle through first back stitch as if to purl and slip stitch off needle. Pull needle through next back stitch as if to knit, leave stitch on needle.
Repeat steps 3 and 4 until only 1 st remains on each needle. Take care to pull yarn carefully through worked stitches periodically. Make sure you do not work your grafting too tight, it should look like a knitted stitch.

Step 5: Pull needle through front stitch as if to knit and slip stitch off needle.
Step 6: Pull needle through first back stitch as if to purl and slip stitch off needle.

Break yarn, weave in yarn tail.

Grafting in Garter Stitch

Place stitches you have been working on the front needle and place stitches from Provisional Cast-On on back needles; break yarn leaving a generous tail, approximately 3 times the length of your work. Thread a tapestry needle with the yarn to the right of the stitches.

Step 1: Pull needle through first front stitch as if to purl, leave stitch on needle.

Step 2: Pull needle through first back stitch as if to purl, leave stitch on needle.

Step 3: Pull needle through first front stitch as if to knit and slip stitch off needle. Pull needle through next front stitch as if to purl, leave stitch on needle.

Step 4: Pull needle through first back stitch as if to knit and slip stitch off needle. Pull needle through next back stitch as if to purl, leave stitch on needle.

Repeat steps 3 and 4 until only 1 st remains on each needle. Take care to pull yarn carefully through worked stitches periodically. Make sure you do not work your grafting too tight, it should look like a knitted stitch.

Step 5: Pull needle through front stitch as if to knit and slip stitch off needle.

Step 6: Pull needle through first back stitch as if to knit and slip stitch off needle.

Break yarn, weave in yarn tail.

INCREASES

LLI(p)

Left Lifted Increase: With left needle, lift head of stitch at base of first stitch on the right needle. Knit (or purl) into lifted stitch.

RLI(p)

Right Lifted Increase: With right needle, lift head of stitch at base of next stitch onto left needle (right leg of stitch at back of needle). Knit (or purl) into back of lifted stitch.

https://stolenstitches.com/blogs/tutorials/lifted-increases

M1 Increases

These increases can be either right or left leaning. If only M1 is specified either can be used.

M1L(p)

Make 1 Left: Insert left needle, from front to back, under strand of yarn which runs between
next stitch on left needle and last stitch on right needle; knit (purl) this stitch through back loop.

M1R(p)

Make 1 Right: Insert left needle, from back to front, under strand of yarn which
runs between next stitch on left needle and last stitch on right needle; knit (purl) this stitch
through front loop.

https://stolenstitches.com/blogs/tutorials/increase-m1r-m1l

Contributors

Carol Feller is a designer, teacher, author, editor, publisher, and yarn producer living in Cork, Ireland. She has published hundreds of patterns and seven books, including *Short Row Knits* (Pottercraft) and *Contemporary Irish Knits* (Wiley). She teaches classes in her studio in Cork city, in local yarn shops, at fibre festivals and knitting retreats, on tours and cruises, and online through Craftsy.com and her website.
Learn more at www.stolenstitches.com

Lucy Hague is originally from Orkney, Scotland, and now lives and works in Edinburgh, where she also regularly performs as a folk musician. She loves to design engaging, intricate patterns with unique twists. Her design work is strongly influenced by Celtic and Pictish art, and she focuses on finding new ways to replicate interlacing Celtic knotwork in cable knitting. She is the author of *Celtic Cable Shawls* and *Illuminated Knits*.
Learn more at www.lucyhague.co.uk

Isabell Kraemer is a qualified dressmaker, knitwear designer, and blogger who has gained a large and dedicated following for her fresh, wearable, and modern patterns. Her designs have been published in *Laine Magazine*, *Amirisu*, and *Vogue Knitting*, and she has produced beautiful designs for *Malabrigo Yarns*, *Quince & Co*, and *Swan's Island*, all in her signature streamlined and contemporary style.
Learn more at www.ravelry.com/designers/isabell-kraemer

Justyna Lorkowska is a former teacher and a knitwear fanatic. She learned her first stitches from her mom when she was a teenager, but she gave up knitting quickly afterwards. Having her first baby brought back her passion with great impact and this time she also started designing knitwear for adults and children. She's been published worldwide in popular magazines, collaborated with established yarn companies, and self-published two pattern books. She lives in Poland and designs knitwear that she would gladly find in her closet: flattering, versatile and seamless.
Learn more at www.letesknits.com

Amanda Schwabe ("Shwah-bee") is a knitting teacher and pattern designer. She loves learning new knitting techniques, fixing outrageous knitting mistakes, and designing wearable garments that are fun to knit. She's passionate about mental health awareness and ADHD. She's an artist whose yarn-bombed horse is in the permanent collection of the Canadian War Museum. She also paints in acrylics and watercolours; yarn and people are her favourite subjects. Amanda lives near Ottawa, Canada, with her husband, their five kids, lots of yarn, and a cat.
Learn more at aknitica.com

Nadia Seaver is a writer, photographer, creative freelancer, and virtual assistant with a focus on fibre arts and cottage gardening. Nadia has worked with multiple Irish knitwear designers and fibre artists in both the roles of copywriter and photographer, and in 2018 was part of the team that launched *Woollinn: Dublin's Festival of Yarn*, curating and presenting the *Yarn in Ireland Panel* in addition to serving as the Press Pool Co-ordinator. Her blog and podcast features interviews with some of the biggest names in the yarn industry.
Learn more at www.cottagenotebook.ie

Karie Westermann does things with wool and words. She is a designer, teacher, and general wool enthusiast. Her work combines her love of storytelling, art, and woolly yarns as she is a big believer in knitting never being "just knitting".
Learn more at www.kariebookish.net

Jennifer Wood began Wood House Knits in 2009. Her designs unite classic and modern styling with beautifully detailed patterns for a contemporary romantic feel. For Jennifer, designing knitwear is a wonderful adventure, allowing her to express her creative impulses and drawing her closer to the Creator of all.
Learn more at www.ravelry.com/designers/jennifer-wood

Woolly Wormhead is a Hat architect, sharing her time between the UK and Italy with her family. With an instinctive flair for unusual construction and a passion for innovation, Woolly is an established designer whose patterns are trusted and celebrated by knitters all over the world. Informed by a background in art and engineering, Woolly sees her Hat designs as sculptural pieces, exploring form through the knitted stitch.
Learn more at www.woollywormhead.com